Sex and the Ultimate Bliss

Sex and the Ultimate Bliss

A Lifelong Quest for
Answers on the Mysteries of Sex

Liberacion Tecson Paragoso

To order additional copies of this book, contact:
Xlibris Corporation
1-888-795-4274
www.Xlibris.com
Orders@Xlibris.com
53998

Contents

Acknowledgment 1
Cover Story.. 3
Introduction 5

Part I—Curiosity: A Game Humans Love to Play
Childhood and Sex.. 11
Sex and Adolescence.. 18
Dating and Sex 24
Sex in Marriage 30
Sex and Infidelity.. 37
Old Age and Sex 43

Part II—Perversion and Addiction: Frailties of Being Human
Perversions and Addictions 53
Prostitution 59
Pornography 66
Sex and Crime 72
Sexually Transmitted Diseases 77

Part III—Anthropology: Who We Are As Human Beings
Sex Culture, Practices, and Rituals 85
Sex Myths and Superstitions.. 93
Insanity and Sex.. 99
Sex and the Brain 105
Human Dignity and Sex 110

Part IV—Theology: The Truth beyond Human Nature
The Creator and Sex... 119
Sex in the Bible 124
Sex and Religion 130
Sex and the Religious Life 137

God Is Love 144

Part V—The Answer: The Seedbed of Sexual Impulse
    The Ground 153
    Temporal Pleasures 158

Part VI—Heaven: The Ultimate Answer
    The Invitation 165
    The Ultimate Bliss 169

Conclusion 175

Selected Bibliography and Related Readings 179

Web sites visited: 183

About the Author 187

Other books by the author: 189

To
my parents
who told me nothing but the truth.

and

to
my children, daughter-in-law and grandchild
who benefit and share the truth

Acknowledgment

It is noteworthy to mention and acknowledge, with my sincere and heartfelt appreciation, those individuals whose ideas and opinions about this topic form an integral part in this book. To name a few, Mr Oriel W. Bacas spent precious time reading and reviewing all the pages and making input on topics about peeping Toms, dating services and web sites, male side on marital sex, dryness and penetration in old age, insanity, and other theories about beginning of life; Atty. Brandon Enad who advised me to be cautious on topics such as perversions, prostitutions, pornography, and sex crimes. Ms. Amabelle Ablan on her insight about some lucid moments of an insane person; and my six sisters, Vive Mamites, Rosita Guidry, Dodie Davis, Zeny Peacock, Cory Bernabe and Maeie Cabije and three brothers, Bing, Flor and Frank, who supplied me with long list of sex legends, myths and superstitions.

More thanks go to my children Lyda Marie and Daryl Mark in their advice not to rush in making this book; my daughter-in-law, Karen, for telling me her childhood experience with a male classmate; and the Internet for saving my time researching instead of going to the libraries.

Above everything, I thank God for making this book possible.

Cover Story

A sexual intercourse as an expression of love
is the *dance of the soul*.

While the physical bodies are connected passionately,
the souls dance in unison as they become one.

This dancing experience of the souls
transcends human passion into blissful union,

and

having experience this together,
their love becomes eternal and divine
as the dance culminates into
the bosom of their creator.

(Page 173, last paragraph)

Introduction

During my childhood years between the ages of seven and twelve, children roamed freely in the neighborhood without fear of being abducted or violated. We climbed trees and ridges in adventure and wandered in places we had never trod. We dipped in the river or bathed under the rain, sometimes naked, as we gathered with our hands drops of rain and splashed them on our faces with frolic and laughter. We did not know the differences between being a girl and being a boy. We just saw each other as playmates ready to spend the day with each other free of worries and concern. Never was there in our minds the awareness that there would be danger or predators lurking behind us. We were like children of the universe: free, adventurous, curious, innocent, and vulnerable. This was what childhood used to be.

During the years of adolescence between the ages of thirteen and nineteen, girls were trained to know the crafts and skills of being a woman, preparing them to become real wife and mother. Boys were told to honor and to respect girls of their age while they searched and chose their best partners in future life. We sweat and quivered with fear when someone from the opposite sex held our hands in public places because it was expected that decent girls never allowed themselves touched by a boy, even holding hands, unless she was already engaged to marry the guy. If a boy liked a girl, he must ask the girl, or her father, permission to visit her in her house or to send her a love letter through the mail or through an emissary—usually a friend or a relative of the girl. Now girls are free to express their interest in a boy. They don't have to wait anymore. They can even visit the boy straight to his bedroom without thinking of decency. They hug and kiss in public, even in school campuses as the other students pass them by. Their sex life is common knowledge.

What was unknown to my friends while I hang around with them was that at age seven, I already saw and knew the truth about how babies were made, who made them, and from what part of the female body the baby came out. It was a little secret that I kept because I was told not to share it with friends or to anyone. This prohibition made me curious why little children were not allowed to see how babies were made and why they could not tell this to anyone. As a child growing up, I had a lot of questions cropping in my head. The more answers I got, the more questions branched out because along the way, I saw contradictions, lies, and inconsistencies in the answers that I got. My curiosity expanded with age. I did not hesitate to ask questions from sources I thought could satisfy my curious mind. I knew sex has always been a very delicate topic to ask for answers, more so if the answers needed must come from the opposite sex. Being a woman and being conscious of what was expected of me, I had to be on guard to avoid being mistaken as a sexually obsessed female. My focus was not on how a person obsessed and passionate about sex could be helped; I left that to the professionals like counselors, psychiatrists, psychoanalysts, and psychologists. It was on what they felt about it and how they viewed sex in their own being—as pedophiles, sex criminals, perverts, husbands, wives, mistresses or lovers, priests, nuns, and other religious leaders, even insane persons and prostitutes. Perhaps it was because of how they viewed sex and what they did with their sex lives that made them who they are. What is in sex that made it so compelling? Why even the old and the aged still crave for this? Are we looking for something beyond sex? Is there such a thing as the ultimate bliss? How do we find it? What is the connection between the ultimate bliss and the experience of sex? Most people say sex is a sin; is it? Did God create sex to make us commit a sin?

I also searched for answers on many audiotapes, books, magazines, movies, videos, and even went as far as surfing the Internet for answers to these questions. I visited pornographic sites for more answers, a conduct unbecoming of a woman, yet I did. The book *The Confessions of St. Augustine,* translated by Monsignor

John K. Ryan, provided me an insight on how St. Augustine, a great sinner—lust included, among other vices—found his conversion and became the greatest saint of the Catholic Church. The audio and videotapes by Christopher West entitled *The Dignity of Man: An Introduction to the Anthropology of John Paul II, John Paul II and Sacramental Sex: What Hollywood Doesn't Know and Your Parents Never Told You,* and *Created and Redeemed: The Universal Message of John Paul II's Theology of the Body* were informative sources that gave me guidance in understanding the human body, its needs, and its purpose. The first encyclical letter of Pope Benedict XVI to his flocks entitled "Deus Caritas Est" (God Is Love) explained the immensity of God's love for us and what each of us must do in response to this experience, particularly the manifestation of love through sexual expression between a man and a woman and how this sexual union of man and woman transformed into the love of God and the love of neighbors.

Further on I was led to the pages of the Holy Bible: in the stories of the creation, fall, and redemption of man; in the songs of Solomon called the "Song of Songs"; in the miracle at the wedding at Cana; and in the conversation between Jesus Christ and Nicodemus, a Pharisee. The many parables and stories of Jesus in the New Testament showed us how much he love his people, including sinners, like when he encountered an angry mob led by the Scribes and the Pharisees, who brought before him an adulteress challenging him to render judgment on her. What Jesus said to them and what he wrote at the time with his finger on the ground would show us what sex was all about and why we could not separate ourselves from it.

The first part explored the mysteries of sex from my childhood experiences to old age. It also chronicled how and when I became curious about sex and my encounters with various people enjoying and abusing it. In the second part, I ventured into the darker side of sex—in the valleys of the dolls, in the forbidden domains of the Internet, and in the annals of sex criminals and serial killers; the third part focused on the complexities and physical aspects of the human nature and the purpose of life; the fourth part dug into the truth about human sexuality: its purpose, and its significance in this life and thereinafter; the fifth part I dared to explain the very source of our own sexuality, its temporal nature, and why it's so compelling; and the last part called us to respond to an invitation that would lead us to our final destination called "heaven"—the place of endless bliss.

My curiosity would have made me a sexually disoriented person; but with the help of a very strong Christian faith, I found the discipline in my attitude, desires, and needs about sex. The many answers that I gathered along the way became my guiding light in understanding human nature and human sexuality—why we were made male and female, and for what purpose we were made so. In this journey I struggled to resist the temptations to enjoy and experience sex in many different occasions. It was because I considered sex as a precious gift from God that I held back my human desires until I found the right person to share this gift with. It was in sharing this gift to someone special that love was born in its truest and purest form: a pure reflection of God's love for all of us, a love that's outreaching and unconditional.

Sex would always be a mystery for all of us, and perhaps by reading this book, you too would find the answers to the many questions you have been asking about.

This book is for you.

Part I

*Curiosity: A Game
Humans Love to Play*

People say curiosity kills a cat,

but one thing about it is that cats could not share with us

what they got out of curiosity, people can . . .

—Anonymous

Childhood and Sex

Playing with my cousin was something to look forward to, especially when her father arrived home after a long absence. He worked as a ship purser, and he only saw his family when the ship docked at the pier. When he got home, he brought for his family a lot of candies, food, fruits, and toys. We would know my uncle was in town because my aunt would share with us the stuffs that he brought for them. My aunt and her family shared a house with my parents. It was she who invited my parents to move their sewing business in the city. They occupied the east wing upstairs, while my family took the west wing and the ground floor. They shared one kitchen located beneath the east wing.

One day my cousin asked me to go upstairs to play with her. After eating, we played hide-and-seek. There was not enough hiding place in the room since the entire space had only a curtain separating the bedroom and the living room. I was the first to hide, so I crawled through the curtain toward the bedroom. I was underneath a bed. I noticed some movements on top of the bed, making it squeaked in a rhythmic fashion. I crawled further toward the edge of the bed to investigate what the sound was all about. I saw my aunt and my uncle both naked facing each other, one on top of the other. Right before my eyes I saw sex in action and in real time. I saw their body movements and their body parts as they made a moaning sound. Suddenly the man collapsed with his weight on top of the woman as if he was dead, yet I still heard both of them moaning intensely as if gasping for air to breathe. I was terrified with what I saw that I hurriedly crawled back underneath and found my way out without being noticed. Without a word to my cousin who was surprised, I rushed downstairs.

My parents were in a sewing business. Every day they were busy making clothes for their customers. They had five people working for them — three seamstresses and two tailors. Downstairs was their workplace. After I settled my breath, I decided to tell my mother or maybe both of them about what I saw, but my fear overwhelmed me. I slowly approached my mother trying to initiate a conversation. "Are you making a wedding dress, Mom?" I asked. "No, this is just an ordinary dress. Why are you asking?" she responded with a question. "No, nothing," I said. "Is there something you need to ask me?" she asked looking me to the eyes. I grabbed a chair and positioned myself sitting beside her, and then I began telling her what I saw upstairs. Before answering me, she made a quick glance at my father, checking if he'd heard our conversation. She raised my chin and whispered, "That's how babies are made, and no one must see that, especially little girls like you. Only adult, married couples do that and that is done in secret." As she talked, I recalled one instance when I woke up in the middle of the night when I saw across my bed a silhouette of two moving figures, the one on top moving up and down as they made a controlled moaning sound. So that explained what I saw: my parents were then making a baby at that time. "Don't ever try to see that again, or the baby would not come." She paused and checked around if someone overheard her lecture. She looked at me again and continued her admonition. "They will surely get mad at you and will never allow you to play with your cousin again. Don't talk about this to anyone, not even to your brothers or sisters." While my mother was talking, my thought was on the candies and the toys that my cousin shared with me. I didn't want to miss them, so I made a decision to stay quiet about it. For months I waited for the baby to come, but it never did. I asked my mother if I was the reason why the baby did not come out because I saw them. She told me to just wait and see, but it never did. I began to doubt my mother.

Some few years later when my family returned to the province, my siblings and I always looked forward to the weekends. Our grandmother would take us, including our cousins, to her house in the farm. We loved to chase butterflies in the field, climb mountains, look for caves, and climb fruit trees. One day I felt sick. I stayed home and spent my time at the veranda of my grandmother's house, gazing at the animals that roamed freely in the yard. Then I saw a bigger duck chasing a smaller one. I was amused. Finally the bigger duck caught the smaller one by the neck and subdued the victim. The bigger duck stepped on top of the victim and tried to balance his weight, swinging from one side to the other like balancing on a tight rope. Then he began lowering his hind part. After a while the bigger duck collapsed on the side, exposing an intestinelike coil. I thought the duck was dead that I shouted for help. "The duck is dead. The duck is dead!" I run to my grandmother who was in the kitchen and tagged her along to show to her what happened to the bigger duck. To my dismay what we saw was that they were already walking away, as if nothing happened. My curiosity was aroused. What was that that I saw? Was that an intestine or something else?

The next day I waited for the ducks to come out. I needed some answers to my questions. I tiptoed to my hiding place, close enough for me to see if they'd do it again. They did it again; and when the big duck collapsed, I immediately grabbed him, and then turned him upside down to locate the intestine. Right when I was about to touch it, my grandmother saw me and told me that I could kill the duck if I pulled it. She told me that that was the genitals of the big duck and not an intestine. She explained to me how the ducks make their eggs, with what I saw, that would then crack and become a duckling. Then I remembered my mother's word some years ago: "That's how babies are made."

In the succeeding weekends that followed, I spent my time gathering pairs of insects and putting them in their respective containers. I wanted to find out how each pair made their little ones. I set up a small laboratory in the barn where I could regularly check the progress of my experiment. I was disappointed because none of the insects did as I expected; instead they all died. On rainy days I gathered frogs, slugs, and worms; and on sunny days birds, butterflies, and other insects. I inspected their genitals, placed them in pairs, and waited for their little ones to come. None of them did. I saw how dogs made their puppies, how goats made their kids; how horses and cows, after a chase on their pairs, had sex. I enjoyed every minute I spent assisting these animals in their struggle to deliver their little ones. I helped remove the slimy filament that wrapped the goat's kids to make them breath. I was so amazed to witness how the horse delivered her colt and the cow her calf. I was warned not to go near a dog when she delivered her puppies; female dogs were possessive of their puppies. I frequently visited nests of hens and watched till the eggs hatched. I also followed up the progress of the two ducks and their eggs. With all these, I considered myself fortunate to know and understand at an early age the real purpose of sex. This learning experience I had in my grandmother's farm became the foundation of my attitude toward sex and the role I would have when I grow up as an adult female and become a mother someday. Little did I know that in my adult years, this childhood experiences would enable me to understand and distinguish animal sexuality from that of human beings.

It was very interesting to observe how different pairs of animals performed their sexual encounters. Some animals attacked each other, as if trying to control or perhaps persuading the other to say yes to the amorous moves. Familiar to me were the dogs. When the female dog was in "heat," she made herself available to the males. I would see five or six males competing in a fight to get the privilege. The female dog usually would select the one with strong muscular features like being of good breed, and most particularly, it was the one that won in the fights—where he drove away the weaker ones. The female dog exposed her hind part to the selected partner, and the partner would smell her hind in circle before doing the copulation. In ducks, the male chased the female as she run around until finally caught. Then the male subdued the female by grabbing her neck as he climbed on her back. Rooster courted the hens like having a dance show displaying for approval. Of all the animals that I marveled the most in their mating behavior were the penguins, as portrayed in the video *March of the Penguins*. Although they didn't have religion, their faithfulness and commitment to their chosen sex partner was awesome. The foreplay before having sex was a model to reckon with, and the attention they gave to their offspring was extraordinary.

There were three occasions where I saw my mother delivered three of my siblings. The first one was at age five, then at age nine, and last at age twelve. My mother always delivered her babies in the house with the aid of a local midwife. Children were prohibited to see how babies were delivered, but my curiosity found me a way to sneak in without their knowing; I was nine years old at that time. I wanted to know where babies got out from their mother's belly. I saw the head of the baby coming first, then the entire body slowly sliding out covered with slimy, sticky, and bloody liquid. I saw what the midwife did to the baby, like cutting the umbilical cord after making a hard spank on the baby's butt to make her cry. I never had fear seeing it because I did not hear my mother screamed with pain. She was only inhaling and exhaling with little moaning and deep sighs. Her demeanor impressed me that I felt no fear of also wanting to be a mother like her. When my turn came to deliver my babies, I had with my first baby sixteen hours of waiting in the labor room until finally before midnight, the doctor decided to make a C-section surgery. A year after I delivered my second child the same way. Though I was already scheduled for another C-Section, the baby came out three weeks earlier after a two-day ordeal of keeping him to wait until the scheduled date. I thought all along that my babies were dead inside my womb because I never felt extreme pain, not like the other woman I saw across my bed. She was like a bull on the loose, crawling under and over the bed, banging and scratching walls, screaming, crying, and cursing her husband and her doctor. I just sat on my bed, wincing quietly every now and then on both occasions.

In my household, the children were growing up free to talk to me about sex without malice. When I found three issues of playboy magazines inside the room of my fourteen-year-old son, I sat down with him and explained that there was nothing wrong with that. I told him I was even glad to find out that he's a real boy. I emphasized to him that there's always the right time and the right reason to do that, but he would have to wait. In the meantime he just had to enjoy his adolescent life. He let me keep the magazines and would ask them from me whenever he wanted to see them (with an alibi of course). When he underwent a brain surgery from aneurysm at age twenty-four, he became worried about his capability to enjoy sex. He talked to me about this, which in return I told him to check it out. He said he could not check it in the hospital because the nurses were coming in every now and then. We requested for a day out, and he checked it in the house. He returned to the hospital satisfied with the result.

Parents play a vital role in the sex education of a child. If done the right way and with proper attitude, children grow up with the right understanding about it. Children are curious by nature, and when they start asking about sex, all we have to do is just be honest and straightforward in giving our answers. They can easily be misled about everything they are curious about. It is for us adult to guide them with full truth and honesty. As they grow up, they will never hesitate to go back for more questions to the person who gave them the right answer for the first time. That person could be you.

When I asked my mother about what I saw upstairs, she did not hesitate to give me the right answer: "That's how babies are made," and I believed her. That experience would have just vanished from my memories, but when I was warned not to tell anyone, I began to ask why. When my children asked us why there were times they could not join us in the bedroom, we told them the truth—we were making another baby. If they asked why the baby did not come, we just told them it was not done right, so we will make again. Imagine how a young child would be making so much noise about when the baby would come. In the process, they would understand.

Today, many of the children are no longer free to enjoy the fun of their innocence. Their free time after school is spent in front of the television. We give our children access to modern gadgets like the computer, cell phone, MP3s, iPod, sex movies, sex magazines, and the like. We see little boys being coached to flirt with little girls; while adults, on the other hand, condone this flirtatious behavior with amusement. We expose our little girls to beauty pageants; put makeup on their tender, innocent faces; and coach them to act like ladies. We love to see ourselves in them. Our behavior is giving them wrong signal with regard to sexuality. They thought it is fun.

Sex, which used to be kept in the privacy of one's bedroom, is now exposed even to little innocent children. My daughter-in-law who was all along innocent about sex during childhood told how her male classmate in grade one made them see what he has by telling the girls eating with him at the school cafeteria to look under the table. What the girls saw was his exposed penis. Many of the girls did not know what it was; they thought it was a toy and they just laughed. What could be in the mind of that little boy to have done such an act with the girls?

Statistics shows some children are killed after being abused by adults—either by strangers or by some person known to them, maybe a neighbor, a relative, or a parent. Take the case of Jon Bennett Ramsey whose murder remains a mystery until now. Who knows the murderer was one of those who saw her in the beauty pageants that her parents love to make of her. Child pornography has become a multibillion-dollar business in the Internet and in some places unknown to the authorities. Why are we doing this to our children? If we adults can't even handle our own sexuality, how much more these little children whose minds and bodies are not yet ready to handle the mysterious underpinnings of sex?

Sometime ago in my neighborhood, there was a guy who I presumed was a pedophile. I regularly saw young boys knocking on his door, and he would let them in. After an hour or two, the young boys would come out giggling and teasingly pushing each other as they walked home. One day while I was getting my mail, the guy passed by while jogging. I initiated a conversation by asking him if he had a problem with the boys I saw knocking on his door. Pretending to be concern for his safety, I asked had the boys disturbed his privacy or did they vandalize his car outside. He replied that he invited those kids to play with his games inside and that he was never bothered by them. So this was how children were lured into the pedophiles' territory: invite them to play games. The pedophile who may have the emotion of a child loves to play with children, but since he has an adult body that has some adult cravings, he plays the game only adult plays—sex. There may have been fun and food inside the pedophile's house that children kept on coming back, plus a cash reward after the fun. It was only when they began asking questions and became a threat that they were being silenced by killing them. During the succeeding weeks, I couldn't find any more reasons to initiate a conversation with him because I noticed he was trying to avoid me. Twice I noticed police cars parked on his driveway and did not see the boys anymore after that. Some few months after, he disappeared.

Sex and Adolescence

My adolescence days were full of fun and adventure. We still hang around with the boys who were our childhood playmates, at the same time entertained secretly our crushes and fantasies on them. In high school two of my close friends got pregnant before graduation, but their parents fixed their predicaments by marrying them before talks about them spread in our town. Another friend disappeared from school, only to be found later—she eloped with her boyfriend after the night she slept with him and had sex. It was unfortunate, though, that the guy did not marry her; instead, she was sent back to the custody of her parents, already pregnant.

In my youthful days, I often hang around with boys. I could even be mistaken as a tomboy because I always wear pants, fly kites, and play fencing with them. Every afternoon we gathered in the plaza across our house and had fun with each other. I knew those boys had a crush on me, but because they knew I was smarter than they were, they just content themselves with my friendship. It was also at this time when boys of my age started to look for answers regarding female body parts. A number of times I caught my male classmates peeping into a hole in the girl's restroom in our school. I reported this to the principal, and they were punished by making them stand under the sun for hours. This male curiosity about the female body continued in adults and even in old age. Like during my college days while I was staying at my aunt's house in the city, one night I heard a sound from the ceiling right above my bed. Suddenly a small saw appeared, making a hole on the ceiling. The guy upstairs must have been trying to see me in my sleep. He was probably hoping that in my sleep my skirt would fold upward and expose my legs, panty, or whatever part that could excite him. In another instance, the landlady next to my aunt's apartment reported that his male lodgers were taking turns peeping on the hole of our bathroom every time a girl took a bath. Also during this time, homosexuality was never an issue in our group. One instance when my brother was using the restroom, a friend peeped on the hole of the toilet he was using. When he saw the peeping Tom, he grabbed him with a punch on his face. The said guy grew up to be a homosexual. I wonder what could be in the minds of these boys acting as peeping Toms.

One time my female friend and I decided to enjoy fresh breeze at the beach as we study for the upcoming government examination for all graduating high school students. From a distance we saw round black objects floating on the sea; we didn't give much thought what they were. Maybe those were dead coconuts which found their way to the sea after a flood. After an hour we saw hands waving as if telling us to go away. We did not know those objects were heads of young boys taking a bath in the sea. Since we did not heed their signals, they decided to just emerge from the sea in spite of our presence. We saw them naked with their erect sex organs exposed as they run towards their clothes. I was not shocked with what I saw, but my friend who must have seen this for the first time screamed as if she saw a ghost. When the boys heard her, they posed before us still naked teasing her much further with the sight.

I was sixteen years old when I had my first boyfriend. He did not pursue me, nor did I pursue him. We were matched by my older sister and her boyfriend in order for them to be free from my watchful eyes as a chaperone to my sister whenever they dated. The relationship did not last long because I found out he was courting my classmate while dating with me. However, when I got my first job three months after I broke up with him, he became interested in reconciling with me; and this time he was like crazy. He became a regular stalker that whenever he saw me walking alone, he would grab me to the dark alley with a forceful hug and a kiss.

One night around ten o'clock in the evening, as I was late getting out from church after an evening Lent prayer with the townspeople; I noticed a shadow behind the grotto of our Lady of Lourdes. When I passed by, a man suddenly grabbed me and pinned me against the back wall of the grotto, hugging me tight and trying to kiss me. The man was my ex-boyfriend. He was reaching for my underwear, at the same time pushing me down. It seemed the alcohol that got into his system fueled his lustful engine with carnal desires, not anticipating that the same alcohol made him physically weak to balance his acts. He easily stumbled down when I pushed him hard. I ran as fast as I could as he crawled on the ground trying to stand again. It did not matter if he was not able to stand after I left him; anyway, he had the ground as his sleeping bed for the night. Somehow the alcohol in his system would not make him remember his embarrassment. From that time on, I never let myself near him. The traumatic experience I had left a very negative impact on my impressions of him and became wary of the other boys of my age. I did not date again until I was twenty-three years old.

My second job was in the city, working as the office secretary—receptionist in an accounting firm. When not so busy with work, my boss would make me type some pornographic materials and compilations of dirty jokes about sex, which he distributed to his friends and associates. He preferred that I do the typing during lunch break when all the employees were out, and I would be alone in the office. Thinking that I was a female and would probably have a lesser reaction to the task, he was comfortable to let me do it for him. Aside from being his secretary, I did extra job helping his children with their homework and assignments or sometimes did grocery with his wife. Oftentimes I picked up his children from school and took them to the office while waiting for their mother who worked as a nurse at the City Health Department. The extra-personal errands I made for his family were of my own initiative because I felt he treated me just like his own daughter.

The materials that I typed every so often were savagely explicit, describing the male's sex appetite like that of hungry wolves or coyote salivating over their food. Although I already saw a sexual act at a young age, I was ignorant about foreplays, the different positions, and the many pervert ways of doing sex. My first reaction was repulsive; I wanted to quit from my office job, but I needed to have money for my college education. I perspired, as if I was trapped in hell; my body was hot, seemingly responding to erotic visualization of the texts, and the discomfort was unbearable. I could not understand my feeling; was it excitement or fear? Because there was no copying machine yet at that time, it took me one whole week to finish thirty copies, sorted and stapled ready for distribution. It was really an ordeal because during the entire week that I was doing the job, the thought about it really disturbed my imagination. Every time I think about it, a specific part of my body tightened, as if wanting for a release. This experience made me very uneasy as I performed my regular office work. The stories were a revelation yet disgusting; I got scared I might be carried away by the excitement and alter my conscience as a consequence. The dirty portrayal of the sex act obfuscated all the beautiful understanding I had about sex during my childhood days. It was no longer for making babies; it was already an expression of animalistic passion. If having sex was for making babies, why those perverted ways of doing it? Were the things that I read necessary ways or techniques to make babies or something else?

None of my officemates knew what I was typing inside my boss' office. He told me to keep that as confidential as possible. This was the second time I was told not to share the sex information I knew with my friends and relatives, just like what my mother told me long time ago. My curiosity wanted to experience the discomfort again, to find out why a person responded this way by just reading the stories. I took home some copies to read, unknown to my parents and my siblings. It was at this time that I understood what masturbation was all about. I wanted to do it, but I had reservation; I was scared of the consequences. I was only seventeen and without a boyfriend.

During my time, I could not share those materials that I kept because none of my friends had an idea about it. I would be degrading myself before them if they'd know I read this kind of literature. One instance my coworkers roasted a female employee, who was always pregnant, with sex questions to which the concerned employee unpretentiously and naively went along with. After every answer she gave, loud and boisterous laughter from everyone filled the entire office. Forgetting I was the only teenager in the office, I joined in the roasting. They asked where I got the dirty joke; they were flabbergasted and could not believe I knew something about sex. I felt so ashamed of what I did; I couldn't find the right words to explain where I got the jokes. From that time on, I became very careful with my participation in situations like that.

Today teenagers are on the same page with their friends. Their sexual encounters are common knowledge, as if they're ordinary and a privilege. To let their friends know, they post their sexual experiences on the Internet with pride. Words like cunnilingus, fellatio, and analingus; words that during my time were never heard of from teenagers, are part of their vocabularies. The rise of teenage promiscuity is commonplace. The chat rooms in the Internet become their outlet in expressing their sexual fantasies with the opposite sex. Their choices of clothing make them look like seductress, exposing cleavage at a young age. Some even posted naked pictures of themselves in the Internet.

Pope John Paul II in his book *Reasons for Hope* (1995) cited that the uncontrolled rise of teenage sexuality nowadays is caused by so much consumerism. From fashion to looks, from magazines to movies, from toys to gadgets, we see sex blended in for more sales and profits. Commercialism in sex results in misconception and delusion of the true purpose and meaning of sex. There is a rapid decline and erosion of morals and values. Teenage pregnancy and abortion are on the rise. Young boys and girls can easily access pornography in the Internet while parents just sleep on them. Some parents even provide condoms when their children go out for a date. Young boys or girls are now dating older partners, and older men or women love to have sex with teenage kids. A big number of teachers were reported to have sexual relationship with their teenage students, which caused them to lose their job in school and ended up being charged with child molestation or rape. Also reported in the media are teenage boys raping babies or little kids or sometimes elderly women who are alone in their homes.

At one time when I was making prom dresses for high school girls in my neighborhood school; while fitting their dresses, I heard them talking about what to do after the party. One topic was about checking in a hotel with their escort. Like an adventure in fantasy land, they looked forward to the excitement of losing their virginity before college. I asked my son if that were true, and he confirmed it. This idea was new to me because prom during my time was only for saying good-byes to all classmates, being the last time we could be together and then part ways for college. Now so much has changed; prom expenses include gowns, shoes, jewelries, perfumes, handbags, rentals of limousines, and hotel booking—only sex after the party is free. What happens after the prom? What if the girl gets pregnant? What about college plans? Statistics showed that four out of five teenage girls are no longer virgins. Could this be the reasons why the statistics for young girls contemplating to be a nun are now rapidly declining?

My mother always told us to preserve our virginity until marriage. She said a husband would regard highly the woman he married if he were the first one to touch her after the wedding. The exposure to sex and the information I had about it during my time were not different from the exposure that the teenagers of today have, but I was always guarded in my language and behavior around the opposite sex. I knew such behavior could possibly mar their impressions of me, much more compromise my desire to be respected by them. I maintained this attitude even when I began dating men. I also advised my younger sisters and friends to do the same. During my time, a girl had to watch her language and behavior before a boy, and should not insinuate or tell a boy that she had knowledge about sex. She would be considered "cheap" and not a good candidate for motherhood or marriage. Though I knew a lot of things about sex, none of the boys I dated knew about it because I was afraid of being misunderstood. They might think my knowledge came from actual experience.

Dating and Sex

The idea of dating with the opposite sex for a sexual encounter probably did not exist in the minds of these creatures known as the caveman and the cavewoman. In comic magazines, a drawing of a caveman holding a cudgel in one hand and in his other hand dragging a woman by her hair would probably lead us to conclude that the caveman immobilized the woman using a cudgel, then dragged her to the cave against her will. Possibly after raping her, he would cut her to pieces for food—a cannibalistic desire for animal flesh. Present times confirm that there are serial killers who eat their victims after raping and killing them—an example, Jeffrey Dahmer. He lured young boys to his apartment, drugged them, raped them, killed them, and then cut the body parts for his food. Another caveman story I recall from high school was that when a cavewoman was in "heat," she would hunt for a man, and then rape him. Knowing their cannibalistic nature, we could also presume that she must have eaten him too. I wondered what she did with her offspring. In present times, we hear stories of women who lure men for sex, kill them, and then mutilate their body parts. They also drink the blood of the victims.

In biblical times, dating was not in practice. When a patriarch of the family saw his son to be ready for marriage, he sent an emissary to the place where they could get a woman for a wife. They would give gifts to the girl's parents such as oxen, goats, lambs and sheep, and even clothing and jewelries in exchange for their daughter. The man and the woman didn't even know each other. Their first meeting was when the woman was sent by her parents to the man's territory. This arrangement looked like the woman was being purchased. Men were in control of the household, and the woman's role was only that of servitude and submission to the desires of the man. Men at that time could have as many wives as they wished. The first recorded arrangement was that of Isaac, son of Abraham, to Rebekah (Gen. 24:1-66).

In the times of the kings and queens, marriages were also prearranged and were limited to those with royal lineage only. Princes and princesses were already matched by their parents, as early as when they were yet babies, with another child of royal blood. Marriage within the royalties, including blood relatives, was their way of keeping control of their wealth and territorial expansion. If a royalty married a commoner, he had to abdicate his throne or rights in the lineage; likewise, he had to give up his inheritance. In this era, men also dominated in the relationship, even ordering the beheading of a queen if she committed shameful acts. The idea of dating never existed during these times.

Dating was said to have originated in Colonial America during the early seventeenth and eighteenth centuries. The book by Beth L. Bailey entitled *From Front Porch to Backseat: Courtship in Twentieth Century America* is a good reading material for this topic.

In the '60s and '70s, dating in third world countries was very much influenced by the movies from Hollywood. Although customs and traditions prevailed in local practices, young boys and girls during this time dated Hollywood style. They would arrange to meet in clandestine places in spite of their parents' strict monitoring of their activities. Parents of the girls would demand that they stay at home and wait for the men to call or visit them. Having a chaperone in a date was still in practice. In dating, it was always expected that the guy foot the bills for his date and the chaperone. Teenage pregnancy was rare, but before talks about someone getting pregnant spread, parents were quick to arrange marriage for their children.

Whenever my father found his daughters seeing boys outside of the house, he would search everywhere to make us go home. One time I received a letter from an admirer; he opened it, got the name of the boy, and reprimanded me not to meet this guy outside of the house. When a guy comes to the house to talk to one of his daughters, he would sit beside him before his daughter could and would start interviewing him of his background. In the end he would tell us that the guy was a distant relative and, therefore, could not date us. My mother was liberal; she would encourage us to go out whenever there was a dance party at the town court.

Now dating takes a different face. Young boys and girls, as early as twelve years old that are not even done with their schooling and could not even raise a family, are now dating. Not only this, sex is even involved in the encounter. Some mothers are even giving their daughter birth-control pills, if they knew their daughter is having sex with her boyfriend. A deviation from the usual norm of only the boys going to the girl's house for a visit, girls now can also go to the boy's house, even going straight to his room. My son is no exception to this situation; girls go straight to his room, but I always tell him to keep the door open whenever his girlfriend is in his room.

Flooded with dating Web sites, the Internet provides access to individuals who are looking for dates. Dating now becomes the key to open doors of opportunities to all people—for sexual encounter, for marriage, for scamming, for abduction, and for crimes. Sexual predators love the Internet. How many news have been reported about missing person who went out to meet another person he/she met in the Internet; but in spite of all the news about missing persons, young boys and girls still continue their adventure in cyberspace. Reality TV shows such as *The Bachelor* and *The Bachelorette* sensationalized dating the modern way. Some viewers, including me, are skeptic that such a show is scripted and the outcome is intended to entertain viewers only. Premarital sex is like ordinary, and to some it becomes a must to determine sexual compatibility. Single bars and clubs, where dating with the opposite sex is expected to happen, proliferated not only in the metropolis but also in small towns. Dating services become a booming business.

At age twenty-three and without a boyfriend, I was graduating college when my landlady arranged for me to meet a guy who was supposed to be my blind date in my ring-hop ceremony. He was a reserved second lieutenant in the army. After the party, we talked and eventually dated until his reserved training for two years ended. He went home to his province. It was rumored though that he was a married man, which he vehemently denied. He said a married man could not qualify for a reserved training in the military. I believed him. We had a number of opportunities to go beyond dating—that was, having sex—but he never asked for it; that alone could be a valid proof that he was indeed a married man, and being aware of this, I was careful in going out with him. He would always rationalize that he honors my ambition of becoming a certified public accountant; that his only desire was to see me realized my dreams. It was noble of him to consider this thing because fate would have followed a different path had we gone beyond. We continued our contact by writing letters for years until I lost him. He sent a telegram congratulating me for passing the licensure, but only that, then silence. Two years after, he called to tell me he was in town and he saw me walked by while he was checking in a hotel near the school where I was teaching. His new job as a medical sales representative of a drug company made him travel extensively. He told me to get a man and settle down, a gentleman's way of putting closure to our relationship. When I asked if he was already married, he did not answer, and then he bade good-bye and hanged up.

My parents' boardinghouse was filled with students from the neighboring provinces, among them young teachers who were finishing their master's degree. Around this time a newly found cousin from the province frequented the place. He was my first cousin, his mother being the older sister of my father. He was already in his late thirties and probably was looking for a wife. He was a licensed engineer and had a very well-paid job in a beer bottling company. I introduced him to all the ladies living with us, but he never found one that he could like. Instead he turned his interest on me. Conservative and overly religious, he always dropped by my workplace to invite me to pray with him in the church before going for a dinner then head home. He never took me to a movie. When he asked permission from my father to marry me, our relationship was severed. I could not go with him anymore. He told my father that since he was going to immigrate to the United States, he would love to take me there as his wife, and no one would know we were cousins. My father was furious; he warned us that if we insisted, he would disown us. He left for the United States but did not marry until I got married first.

A year after my cousin left for the United States, I dated a seventeen-year-old guy who was staying in our boardinghouse.

He was enrolled in nautical science to become a seaman someday. Every afternoon, he picked me up from work, and we walked our way home together. Our relationship continued until I became a teacher in the school where he was enrolled. We walked to and from school together during schooldays. There were two instances where we would have been carried away by our passion, but our inexperience, being our first, didn't let us through. We were always interrupted by the other students staying in the boardinghouse. In another time after seeing a movie, he pulled me to the restroom and tried to have sex with me in a standing position. Although I read about different sexual position from the pornographic materials my boss asked me to type, I did not believe having sex standing was possible. I was so scared to experience it because the restroom is a public place. What if other restroom users would see us? That would be a big talk in school where I was teaching, the movie house being adjacent to the school. I pulled my boyfriend out to stop him. Our romantic relationship was cut short because martial law was declared in our country. If not for that event, we would have been tempted to try it again and probably get myself impregnated. Since all the schools and universities were closed, he went home to his province. When the school reopened, he did not come back to finish his studies; instead, he joined the US Navy. He never wrote a letter nor made an attempt to contact me through his returning town mates who stayed again in the boardinghouse. I presumed he was not interested in me.

My first year of teaching was a big challenge for me inside the classroom and outside. Two of my students openly expressed their crushes on me: one I would meet again thirty-five years later, already holding a prestigious office in the city government. Aware of the school policies and the code of ethics in the teaching profession and its implications, I shove aside their hero-worshipping of me. Finding passion and dedication in my teaching career, I was able to move on with my life after being hurt by a previous love affair with a young guy. During my probationary period, I got three excellent evaluation reports for each year from my students. I stayed in the school for fourteen years until my family left for the United States.

Another guy, a former student, pursued me. During the time we were dating, I noticed that the guy he introduced to me as his cousin was always going with us wherever we go. They seemed to have a very special relationship. One day I went to his rented room to pick up the homework of my students that he accidently took with him. When I arrived there, the door of his room was half open. I slowly peeped in so as not to disturb him if in case he was sleeping. To my surprise I saw him and his said cousin both naked; he was lying flat on his chest with his butt raised a bit upward; his cousin, on a squatting position holding his loins, was hunching on his butt. I moved aback and took a deep breath. I waited for more minutes, giving them time to finish what they were doing, and then I knocked. They were already dressed when they opened the door. I took the papers and hurried to school for my classes. He offered to go with me, but I told him he didn't have to. Maybe this guy was in search of his true identity that's why he tried a heterosexual relationship, or maybe he kept a heterosexual relationship to cover his skin, the fact that at that time gay men were still hiding in their closets. It was just unfortunate that I discovered his secret by accident. I broke up the relationship but did not tell him what I saw. He did not stop begging for reconciliation for months, following me everywhere. During that time, my coteachers arranged a matchmaking game on me to a fellow teacher who was just promoted to the deanship in the Liberal Arts Department. When the guy proposed marriage, although we never dated, I gave love a gamble; I said yes. The gay guy threatened to disturb my wedding, but when I spilled before his face the secret he was hiding from me, he did not make good his threat; he just let the curtain fell and made an exit.

Sex in Marriage

The invitation card that the chairman of the English Department made for my wedding had these few lines to begin with: "The odds are from ten to zero but time and a lot loving can change all that . . ." Being one of the matchmakers, he would know the high probability that this marriage would encounter a lot of adjustments and uncertainties. My husband and I barely knew each other in spite of the fact that we were working at the same school. He was on his seventh year with the school, while I was on my third year when we settled down in marriage. He had his own circles of friends, myself not one of them, and just recently broke up with his girlfriend, another coteacher. On my part, I just broke up my relationship with the gay guy I dated and also received a call from a long-lost boyfriend who advised me to settle down. If we didn't take that as the reasons for hurriedly settling down, perhaps it was the age. I was twenty-nine; he was thirty-two. Marriages between two consenting adults happened for so many reasons. One situation could be that because of premarital sex, the woman got pregnant, forcing the man to settle down in marriage, even if love was still in question. Some men marry for financial security, like finding the woman to be wealthy or influential, that even if love did not exist or that the woman is not pretty, a good-looking guy would take her for a wife. But a majority still marries for love's sake; and this one, over all the other reasons, has the higher probability of having a lasting marriage.

At the time when we were preparing for the wedding celebration, a sore-eyes epidemic was spreading in town. I was one of the casualties right on the day I was supposed to walk down the aisle; however, the makeup artist concealed it with her expertise. Because this kind of disease was very contagious, we cancelled our honeymoon and just went home after the wedding reception. In the house he slept on the couch, while I slept in the bedroom. It took almost two weeks to have my eyes cleared.

I could not account how the first time I had sex went. It happened on one of the ordinary nights when we already went back to our teaching jobs. Experienced he was with so many women, he probably could tell I was a virgin. The many things that I knew earlier about sex, the pornographic materials I got hold of before marriage, did not help. I was still scared to give myself to a man. To me sex as an expression of love in marriage is the most profound of all sexual encounters; without love it is just an obligation or lust. I knew love doesn't come so quickly just because we walked down the aisle together. We had to learn to trust each other and made ourselves ready to put the marriage vows to work in the relationship. Having married to a man I had not dated, my first sexual encounter could then be considered as an obligation or lust. When I decided to settle down in marriage, I was ready to make sacrifices and was willing to do whatever I could to make my marriage work. In conflicting moments during marriage, real motives for marrying a person could surface as words of regrets and resentments on each other were vented out. My marriage for one was not an exception to this kind of situation and in spite of this realization, I stayed in the marriage with the hopes that somehow, someway, and someday my marriage would work.

Marriage in Christian teaching is one of the seven sacraments instituted by Jesus Christ. I considered my marriage vows sacred and a commitment to hold it for better or for worse, to withstand the challenges of having a family. I may had made mistakes in making hasty decision to marry, but to walk away from this commitment; more so if children were already involved, could be considered an immature and irresponsible act. Personal and emotional adjustments in marriage could take over time; much more if one or both couples still had attachments to their parents and relatives. I did not have problems with my parents and relatives because they never took sides whenever there was a conflict. In fact every time I told them of my problems, they admonished me only because they did not want my husband to know that they knew of the conflict.

My determination was tested when my eldest child was diagnosed with a malignant bone cancer at the age of ten. Trying times like this should have made marital bonds stronger as the couples faced together the emotional and financial aspect of the problem. This was not the time to isolate oneself in a bubble where one could not reach the other for an emotional support. With all my emotional strength and faith in God and without whining, I tackled the problem. What sustained me to stay in this marriage was my commitment to my vows and the thought that other marriages had also their own kind of trials and tribulations much heavier than what I had. In situations like this, sex took its toll.

Performances and satisfaction in marital sex depend upon the couples doing it. Some couples have sex before sleeping, while others prefer after they are rested, mostly at three o'clock in the morning. A fellow teacher confided to me that whenever her husband didn't want to have sex, he would put a pillow in-between them as if he was giving her a message that sex was not available for the night. The practice was rather unfair for her because if she were the one who didn't want sex, she could not put a pillow in-between them; her husband would surely cross the border by all means.

Another wife could not understand why her husband suddenly became moody after they had sex, as if he was angry something was taken from him—like his vitality was being sucked out. Lovemaking really tired a man mostly, and this could be the explanation why he became moody after sex. If this happened to a man who had inadequate understanding of sex, sooner or later sex would take its toll. A sex therapist confirmed this to be true in some men, and women should not be offended by this. Researchers even reported to have studied men and women, including married ones, having post sexual depression.

In the faculty room of the school where I was teaching, I could hear conversation between husbands talking about what they expect of their wives when it comes to lovemaking. One husband commented that he'd be turned on more often if his wife didn't take a bath. The smell of her unwashed body part just made him sexually aroused. Conversely, some husbands or wives were easily turned off by their partners who didn't have physical hygiene. Their libido just turned sour when they smelled something awful coming from their partner. When I asked a close relative what could have been the cause of his divorce; why his wife had an affair, his answer was that his wife didn't want him to touch her because his fingers were blackened with grease since he worked as a car mechanic. Over all most couples preferred their partners to smell clean during the lovemaking.

Another couple, a distant relative, found pleasure by having a fight or scuffle before having sex. Jealousy and control of the other was the theme of their game, like these were their methods of arousing the other. Hurting the other verbally and physically preceded amorous romancing and apologies. After hurting his wife, the husband would make up his offenses in a very passionate performance which the wife also responded with equal fiery passion. This behavior looked like a sadomasochistic expression of marital sex. After the act, the couple could be seen refreshed and revitalized like new lovers. Everyone in their family already knew what followed after the scuffle, so nobody cared whenever they fight.

Other couples have fun before having sex. Their foreplay includes all kinds of touching, flirting, even teasing each other. They enjoy talking to each other as they share the task of preparing their favorite meals in the kitchen. They play their favorite music and dance with it. They arrange a candlelight dinner and with some wine. They take a shower together, bathe and massage each other, then make themselves ready for the bed. After the sexual act on any place they choose—bed, couches or wherever, they talk about the experience before sleeping. This is a romantic way of expressing marital sex, and there is no reason why other couples cannot do this.

There are married couples who use sex as a reward or a punishment to each other. For a husband to use his wife's effort to please him in their sexual acts as lewd, attributing this to her as a shameful character, calling her a slut, like presuming she's experienced and expert in lovemaking with others before marriage, is like making a crack in their marriage vow, which is to cherish and to hold each other's dignity. Using this as a tool to debase her in times of marital conflict is a grave sacramental injustice to their marriage and can never be forgiven. Whatever they do in the privacy of their marital bed is theirs to savor and enjoy. What kind of a man is he who would not appreciate and enjoy the pleasure he gets from his wife, unless of course this man has some issues with regard to his own sexuality—maybe he is gay or bisexual and has less regard to a woman who happens to be his wife?

During my daughter's birthday party, I overheard one of my male guests telling the other men around him, as they were gathered at the terrace talking about politics, women and sex, that he could appease his raging, angry, or crying wife with sex because, according to his statement, women are sex hungry. After hurting his wife, he would perform sex with her until she calmed down. It is selfish for a husband, who thinks this way, to force sex with his wife who is still hurting and crying after an altercation. Maybe the wife just gave in to avoid being abused again if she turned down his sexual advances. There may be some truth that some women are sex hungry, but the way it was said was condescending. It is true that men and women are equally the same in their sexual appetite, but viewing a woman this way is sexist. It was also at this occasion that I overheard a male guest telling the other male guests how he wished he could make love with his wife anywhere in their house like on the couch, on the carpet, on the kitchen table, and at anytime like in the morning or in the afternoon; but his wife wanted only at night and on the bed. When the evening came, he forgot about it; or if he remembered, the desire was no longer as exciting as when he wanted it earlier. Relationship between a man and woman is complimentary, and this is well expressed in marriage.

In biblical times, the man and the wife-to-be were complete strangers to each other, yet they never had issues on adjustments and in-laws. A man gets a wife by offering to the father of the woman a portion of his treasure: cash, livestock, jewelries, clothing, piece of land, which in a sense could be considered a purchase transaction. It was a necessity that a man gets a wife to increase his tribe and to have an heir that will continue and preserve the family. We would be asking how their sex life was. How did they manage their relationship? People at this time lived by obeying the commandments of God, their patriarchs, and elders. In marriage a husband honors his wife, and the wife submits to her husband. With this simple formula, they live in harmony and eventually learn to love and respect each other. This used to be the setup in marital relationship—a woman embodied refinement, culture, and virtues. Her role in a relationship was to provide man children who would be heirs to the wealth that he acquired through hard work. She waits for her husband, takes care of the children, makes the house clean, prepares food for the family, and provides him a pleasurable sex. Now this role had been modified to fit the demands of time. Women gain equal rights and the freedom to express herself, but they lost the respect and admiration of men. In places like the United States where women's right are well guarded and defined, a wife can sue her husband for rape if he forced her to have sex with him. In other places, particularly in third world countries, it is still a man's world. Women have to submit to the desires of their husband, even if it is against her will. Families don't plan how many children to bring in the household. I remember one instance when our oldest sister came to visit us and she was pregnant with her tenth child, my mother made a comment that made her cry. I understood why my mother commented because she had fourteen children, and it was difficult for her to care for all of us and for sending us all to school. It was said that refusing a husband his sexual rights was a mortal sin; so the wife just give in and bear the consequences.

The idea of getting married has declined so much nowadays that most cohabitation just became self-serving. In our culture, it is always the man who makes a marriage proposal, but who would think of doing it now when sex is freely available without strings attached? If one found the other useless after years of living together, finding another as a replacement is not a problem. The attitude of selfishness, not willing to make sacrifices for the other, and free sex just make marriage obsolete and irrelevant. Wait until old age and we will find that being alone and without someone to care for us is the heaviest toll we pay for our selfishness. The caregivers in the retirement homes and the nursing homes cannot give the tender, loving care that a family member can. I have seen sad faces of old men and women sitting by themselves in those homes. If we were to read their minds, it could be that they were wishing that if only they could relived their lives, they would choose to live it again with someone in marriage and build a family.

In a society where women demand equal rights with men, the sacredness of sex in marriage gradually diminishes its importance and significance. Women find fun in flirting with men, regardless of their civil status, to spice their stressful life in the workplace; and men, on the other hand, welcome this behavior with open hands. In the olden times, women were shy in expressing their interest in men, but not now.

Sex and Infidelity

When I learned that my aunt was only a mistress of my uncle, I began asking questions why. Instead of asking my mother for answers, I went straight to my aunt. Indirectly, I asked her why I seldom see my uncle and where he stayed whenever he was not in her house. My aunt was straightforward with her answers. She told me he had a family in the province. I did not ask further, but that didn't mean I was satisfied with her answer. I asked my mother the story of her life, the whereabouts of her husband, and why they were separated. I found this out when my uncle came to my parents' house one day looking for my aunt. At that time my aunt was hiding from him with another man.

Infidelity happens for so many reasons, and it always goes with sex. Sex is a "heavenly" experience for the unhappy, unfaithful married individual, since it is used to fill-in the void or emptiness he/she felt in marriage. In most cases, the relationship is for a short period only, sometimes on and off, but seldom permanent. However, there are extramarital affairs that last until old age but only very few of them. One remote cause is wrong marriage. My mother told me the story of my aunt's love life. During World War II, my aunt already found the love of her life and was planning to marry him. The problem was that their brother, a soldier, disapproved of the relationship. The guy was not from their place and was also a soldier temporarily assigned there. There was another man, a businessman who went crazy for her, who befriended their brother so he could marry her. Thinking of a financially secured future for her, their brother forced her to marry this guy. On her wedding day, their brother locked up her boyfriend so he could not disrupt the ceremony. I asked my mother why she bore a child with her husband if she never loved him. She said my aunt was raped by her drunken husband on the night after their wedding. After giving birth, she ran away to the city, leaving the child to the care of my mother, and lived a loose life hanging around with the American GIs; she got a son with one of them. After the war, she was told by a common friend that her boyfriend, the soldier, died. Then she met my uncle, but he was a married man.

We would be wondering why some individuals search for pleasure outside of marriage. Should we say sexual incompatibility? How do we measure compatibility? What about boredom of being in the marriage for a long time and just need a break by flirting with others—like having an emotional fling? In spite of being married, an emotionally immature woman who thinks she is young by denying her real age, who believes she is pretty and attractive to the opposite sex could also invite extramarital affairs. Her behavior sends wrong signals to men who are pleasure seekers. Weakness in the flesh is an issue to some individuals whose concept of love is based on looks only. Flirting and flattering with the opposite sex is their way of seeking compliments in return. Doing this kind of game to a married man or woman seems a challenge to them. It is a boost to their self-esteem if they could manipulate the opposite sex using their looks. Without regard as to how many marriages they break, being labeled as a playgirl or a playboy is to them a medal of accomplishments. I had a classmate in high school that had this kind of thinking. She loved to be surrounded by the boys after school. Even up to this time, she still dates men unknown to her husband.

Overzealous friendship between a male and a female oftentimes leads to extramarital affair. It could happen anywhere, anytime, when one individual shares in confidence his or her personal problems. There is always the tendency to be concerned and to give advice, which if done regularly may lead to an emotional entanglement. A person's ego is always flattered when somebody asks for an advice.

A coteacher who was a loving husband and a good provider to his family, who everyone thought would never be involved with his student, got entangled to an affair when a smart student's grade began failing in his subject. In his effort to help out the student, he devoted time for her after the class. At first they could be seen in the classroom before everyone's eyes, giving her advice what to do with her boyfriend and her parents and how not to affect her grades. Then they moved to the cafeteria, still within sights by everyone. Conscious of the scandal the scene might make in the school campus because the student was sometimes seen crying and he was seen wiping her tears, they changed venue. It became a secluded cafe outside of the school, then finally to a hotel. The meeting continued for a long time in a clandestine manner until the student got pregnant. Claiming the child to be his, he found himself responsible for their well-being that eventually he rented an apartment for his other family and frequented there or even slept there when there was trouble (minor spat) with his wife. Scenarios like this are very common in the workplace: office mates helping out each other in their personal lives, then unknowingly become emotionally and physically involved with each other.

I had a neighbor who, to everyone's eyes, was ideal until one day the wife came knocking on my door with a problem. She found out her husband was having a mistress. Before she could tell me her problems, I already had the idea that it has something to do with fatal attraction. She was overweight, old-fashioned, and unattractive. Her husband was sleeping with a young voluptuous, seductive, and an attractive woman. She was a turnoff; the other woman was a turn-on. I did not consider issues on temper and character because I know she was a patient and a loving wife and even a doting mother to her children. It could be possible that her husband was experiencing the so called midlife crisis. When I met her again twenty-five years later, she and her husband were still together enjoying their retirement days.

Midlife crisis, more obvious in men after forty than in women, is also one of the causes of infidelity. In this situation, men tend to act like young again by wearing tight denims pants, leather jackets, smelling with perfume, and more often seen hanging around with younger women and riding a Harley Davidson motorcycle. When I asked my husband about it, he said that is true because at this particular age, men are beginning to experience a decline in their virility. To check this is to try sex with younger women—it makes one feels young again. This fling is only temporary because these men eventually would come to realize that younger women are only interested in their money. Once the resources are gone, the thrill and the younger woman are gone too. The danger here is when the wife does not understand and divorce the husband instead. He could lose his family and his finances. I know a number of men who underwent this so called midlife crisis. After having so much money from their retirement, they start hanging around with younger girls, spending lavishly here and there. Some men find romance in the chat room of the Internet, spending hours of expressing love notes to the person in the other computer and when their wife finds out, that's when they realize they have a family.

Newspapers are often flooded with news about unfaithful married man or woman committing crimes by hiring a killer to eliminate their husband or wife so as to free them from their marital bonds. Domestic violence, indifference, and lack of communication in marriage could trigger the possibility of extramarital affairs. So many women who run away from home because of these are easy prey and could be lured into a relationship that would only aggravate their situation. What kind of man would want to be involved in a relationship with a woman whose husband is violent? The last thing a man could wish for himself is to be in confrontation with a violent man. This kind of man would surely walk away from her, thus only adding salt to her open wound.

Estranged sweethearts who truly loved each other, separated by circumstances, got married to a different person, and met again after long unexplained years of silence could easily rekindle their relationship. If one of them has an unhappy marriage and tell the other about it, the affection that was buried in the past could turn into sympathy and willingness to comfort the other. There would be a possibility of them becoming unfaithful to their husband or wife.

When I decided to have a long vacation in my hometown, my intention was to find something that could make me enjoy the remaining years of my life, like volunteering in a charitable cause and stay there for good. But the thought that my first grandchild was on the way, I became ambivalent in my decision. During the early weeks after my arrival, I learned from a colleague that one of our students just got promoted to a very prestigious position in the government. I knew this guy as one of those young boys who had a crush on me during my early years as a teacher in college. Since I would be staying there for six months, I opted not to give him a call to congratulate because I was anticipating that if his affection rekindled, there would be ample time for him to get connected romantically with me. A week before I leave back to the US, I left a message and a contact cell number of my coteacher to his wife's secretary, congratulating him for his achievement. When he got the message, he went around looking for the address my coteacher gave him. He found my place, and we talked about each other's past, including those days when he was pursuing me. The information he gave that he married late at forty-one made me wary about his activities as a bachelor. He must have been enjoying life with women of any kind all those days and never thought of marrying. Although he did not mention to me anything about his marriage, his friends hinted to me that he had a problem. We dated, sort of, and had fun during those few remaining days, but only as a former teacher and a former student finding each other after thirty-five years. He did some romantic advances, though, but I declined, owing to the fact that I was not looking for sex. However, I was entertaining a funny scenario to amuse myself, that supposing I'd do such, like going with him to a hotel for sex, how would I look going naked before a man not my husband with my bulging, saggy belly, deflated breast, and varicose veins on thighs and legs—these are turnoffs. The thought alone of having a forbidden sex might start his engine running, but before he could take off, seeing these things would just give him a nosedive. It was also risky to have sex with a promiscuous man who had been involved with many different women all his life. What if in the process I would get the germs of a misguided sex. Besides I am not young enough to receive a compliment from an old guy; the fact that he too was already in his "seniors" year. Whether older men accept this or not, dating or having sex with younger women is better than with an older woman.

When I arrived home, without his asking of my activities, I told my husband about the short escapade that I had. At first he was forgiving, but in the succeeding days, his insecurity and jealousy began to surface. When I went back to my province six months later, he became suspicious I would be seeing the guy again. I did not. When I arrived at the hotel where I was staying, I gave his name to the front-desk clerks and instructed them to deny my presence. The telephone operators of the hotel were also given the same instructions. Infidelity is a matter of discipline. No matter how troublesome one's marriage could be, entanglement with another person that involves sex is not a game; or if it is a game, it is a very, very serious game because emotions and reputations are at stake. It only takes one stupid mistake to ruin a marriage. If a person is unhappy in his/her marriage, infidelity is not the answer; divorce or legal separation is.

Old Age and Sex

Every day when we commuted to work or to school, we always took a ride on a public transportation called a "jeepney." To board the vehicle, passengers climbed the back passage, holding the two metal bars mounted on each side, and then took a step on the metal ramp. Passengers then took a seat facing each other. I always took the first seat near the passage so I could easily take off when I reached my destination. Ladies at that time wore miniskirts, which naturally exposed the thighs when seated. Every time an old man boarded the vehicle and upon climbing onto the vehicle, instead of taking hold of the metal handle of the vehicle, the old man would grab my thighs for his support without even apologizing. He took it as a privilege because he's an old man. Not only that, when the driver made a sudden brake, instead of holding the metal bar mounted on the ceiling above his head, he would jerk sideways and put his hand for support on the thigh of the woman next to him and intentionally rubbed his elbow to the chest of the woman. Just imagine how we grinned when this thing happened to us. We could only wish and pray that no dirty old man would take a ride with us or that the seats were already taken.

Age, as the saying goes, is just a number; and probably this is said as a justification that in sex there is no such thing as old age. Old age is divided into three groups: those that are (1) physically fit through regular workout, excellent eating habits, no illness, and can still perform regular sexual contact—though less; (2) sickly, no exercise, and still wishing to have sex; (3) practical, accepts their sexual deficiencies, prefers company over stress, and happy by just being old. Only very few belong to the third group. Majority still thinks sex is essential in order for them to live longer.

Knowing that majority in older people belongs to the first and second group, plus the supply of retirement money, the commercial world finds a good market for promoting their products to them. Consumerism invades their lives. The business of Viagra (sildenafil), Cialis, Levitra, and all kinds of sexual aids, tablets, cream, lotion, and patches becomes a multibillion-dollar enterprise. These pharmaceutical and cosmetics companies are willing to pay expensive advertisement and the media to promote their products. Old people are brainwashed with the belief that if they used their products, sex at old age is just as pleasurable as when they were still young. At old age, men work hard for erection and penetration, or desperately wish for orgasm. If a sexual act per se is already stressful, how much more stressful it is to desperately work hard for it, yet it doesn't happen, add to this the aging aching body. Another factor that makes it more difficult is when the woman experiences dryness and without lubricants; penetration becomes more problematic. Also without stimulation older women have difficulty reaching a climax. Just imagine the frustration of wanting it yet not having it. If sex therapists are concerned about the well-being of their aged patients, they should include the psychological aspect of having sex at old age. To use sexual capabilities as a panacea to old-age depression only aggravates the depression. It is misleading to say to old people that sex keeps their bodies healthy and young, that sex is an exercise that prolongs life. These are all commercial slogans intended to encourage old people to buy their products, thinking these products really works. We ache everywhere in our bodies; our heartbeats are catching up our breath; our legs can hardly make a step to the bed, then we think of having sex before sleeping? This reminds me of a joke that my father used to tell his old friends about: Two seniors, ages seventy-five and seventy, checked in a hotel for a honeymoon. Maybe because of eating too much in the wedding reception, the man after trying hard to have sex had a diarrhea instead. He told his new wife: "Had I known you could cause indigestion, I shouldn't have married you." The woman answered: "Well, had I also known you would only make me a toilet bowl, I too shouldn't have married you."

When I was still young, I thought sex stops at old age, meaning old people don't have sexual intercourse anymore. Even without asking, the physical features alone of old people would lead us to think that their weak, fragile bodies cannot handle anymore the stressful activities of sex. When I heard stories about old people still talking about sex or still doing sex with their partner, I just considered that as mere reminiscence and wishful thinking; as everyone says, "The spirit is willing, but the body cannot." But when my eighty-year-old mother-in-law told me that her ninety-year-old husband accused her of having an affair with another man just because she would not let him have sex with her, my impressions were changed. In another instance, I saw, as I passed by, my own father, then in his seventies, sitting by the window, flipping the pages of a JC Penny catalog and touching the bras and underwear of the ladies in the pictures. For a while I stood by the window spying about what he was doing. I saw him feeling his fingers over the pictures as his other hand tacked in between his thighs, checking for an erection. I told my mother about this, and she just giggled and laughed, telling me she knew that even before I told her.

Men are programmed to the idea that they are the active participant in a sexual act and, therefore, have the role of providing pleasure to his sex partner. This is evident when they gather exclusively; their common topic is always women, sex, and how they score with it. So as men aged, this notion remains in their subconscious mind that even at old age, they are still challenged to prove that their sexual prowess does not ebb. When my family moved to a new address, my new neighbor who was living alone came to introduce himself to us. He told his age to be fifty-six, even though we did not ask. Five years after, he got a wife from China who also became our friend. One day she came to our house unloading her discovery about her husband. He told her in their exchanges of letters while she was still in China that he was fifty-six years old. When the time came when the wife had to fill in the necessary documents for her citizenship, she found out her husband was seventy-six when they were married. She was so disappointed, but she just decided to stay to serve him as a show of gratitude for taking her and her son to the United States. Eventually though, they divorced because the man was paranoid that his wife was only after his wealth and would take a younger man when he dies. He was the one who divorced his wife.

Women, on the other hand, consider outward appearances as something they have to maintain so as not to drive men away as they aged. It is not so much about how to perform in bed but more on how she looks that could sexually arouse men. A healthy woman though old can still response in a sexual intercourse. Their insecurity is when their husband becomes sexually attracted to a younger woman. A very close friend whose husband was having an affair suddenly became very seductive with her choice of clothes and would often talk to us about her imaginary admirers who were young and good-looking. According to her telltale, some young men flirted with her by giving her red roses to symbolize her youthful beauty. This kind of behavior could only be interpreted as her way of trying to be attractive to her husband—by constantly telling herself that she is still attractive. It is a sad fact that after years of being a wife and a mother, some older women neglect their own personal image that sometimes could cause impotency of their husband, much more if the neglect is about care for their bodies and appearances. They become a turnoff. This explains perhaps why one of my aged aunts could be heard complaining about my uncle not taking a bath for months. He said his skin dries up from regular bath; she said he has a foul smell. Because their children were all married and lived in their new homes, they have in their old house extra room for each to sleep on, but the husband complains she has become indifferent and probably is having an affair. It cannot be denied that as the body ages, it emits some odorous smells that are offensive to other people's nose; how much more if an old person does not take a bath regularly. In a relationship even at old age, personal hygiene and personal appearance must be maintained by the couple.

Foreplays and romantic innuendoes among older people are oftentimes taken for granted or totally set aside because to them these things can't help anymore prepare their bodies to the main event. It could be that such foreplays and romancing each other only waste their time, and they have to catch up with the much-sought erection. I remember a fellow teacher whose husband was twenty years older than she was. In the middle of her viewing a video in their house or doing the regular chores in the house, her husband would suddenly call her to hurry up because he felt like he had an erection, or she would miss the chance to have an intercourse. This situation is also confirmed to be true by a close relative whose husband is very much older than she is. In the middle of her sewing clothes or in the middle of her sleep, her husband would hurry her up to catch up his erection or lose it.

I always visit a retirement home, owned by a customer, to deliver food that she regularly orders from me. The residents are aged people who are still healthy but are placed there by their relatives, rather than being left alone without somebody watching them in their own homes. What I learn from the caregivers is that the male and female residents are still romantically engaging each other and are oftentimes caught having sex. Because I regularly visit the place, they become my friends; oftentimes stay for a while to chat. The residents seem to be upbeat in demeanor whenever we talk about their romantic lives and sex. I take the opportunity to ask how they feel about it. Is it the same as when they were still young? What I gather from their answers that I thought to be true—those who had pleasant experiences with sex during their youth had the same attitude with sex in their old age; on the other hand, those with unpleasant experiences tend to show no interest at all. Hostility in old age could also be caused by inability to have sex by either partner. Irritable verbal remarks with each other are common in marriages that stayed together in spite of domestic abuses. A friend once told me that her father-in-law always hit his wheelchair-bound wife even in the presence of their relatives. It could be that he was frustrated for not having sex with his wife anymore. In some couples, old age is the time of life when they unload against each other their gripes and resentments that have been accumulated through the years. They are easily irritated with each other; all they see are the faults and imperfections of the other. In the words of their children who are caught "in-between", they are fighting like cats and dogs; always growling at each other.

Old age is best experienced when the husband and wife spend their retirement days together reminiscing the sad and happy moments they had during their younger days. I am a witness to a relationship that surpassed the tests of hardship and suffering in the person of my parents. They produced fourteen children in their marriage, two died during infancy. There was a very touching moment I saw with my parents that I failed to capture with a camera. My sickly father was seated on a wheelchair with one leg on top of the other; my mother was kneeling in front of him, trying to fit in his socks. I knew my mother had a heart problem and high blood pressure, but she still managed to service the needs of my father. I was moved with pride, thinking how fortunate my siblings and I are being raised by two loving parents who not only loved and cared for their children but also loved and cared for each other. During the time when my father was bedridden with cancer and was waiting for his time to go, he always asked my mother to lie down beside her as he stretched his arm to hold her head. Before sleeping, they would talk about their life together, including sex, how they worked hard to raise twelve children and being able to send them all to college. My mother was a seamstress and my father a tailor. My mother, a fun-loving woman, one day told us that as they lay together in bed, she would touch the private part of my father and teased him about it. How they giggled together, recollecting the different instances of their lovemaking, including those embarrassing moments. What was missing in their relationship, which was the ability to perform sex, was being filled-in with the loving memories of their youthful days. To them it was like having sex but in a different way.

Because most people equate love with sex, express love through sex, we think sex is the answer to our insecurities and loneliness at old age. I oftentimes heard children limiting their widowed or separated parents from having a relationship again. Remarks like "Dad you're too old for sex, why take a wife at your age, or Mom you are wasting your time with an old sickly person, why marry that guy?" Children should take into consideration that they have their own lives to take care about. What we really are looking for at this time of our life is the feeling of being loved, being cared about, and being thought about by someone. What could be in the heart of a lonely old man who lost the woman in his life through death or divorce? What could also be in the heart of a lonely woman who lost the man in her life on the same reason? This is why married couple, while still young, should value relationship above all other things because when our bodies can no longer express love through sex due to old age or sickness, recollecting those fond memories of the past can fill in the void of loneliness and emptiness. If their younger days were spent with violence, physical and verbal abuses, and emotional debasement, who would like to talk about it in their old age? Probably they already have gone their separate ways and just spent their "sunset" days in obscure solitude.

In our younger days, we worked hard to save some extra money for retirement. What we did not do or just did not care to do is to save our relationship with our husband or wife for an enjoyable retirement days, build up a nest of pleasant and loving memories together. How romantic would it be to play your wedding song and dance with it again, even if the knees are already shaking? How sweet would that be to recall them at old age, like "Did you remember on our wedding honeymoon, darling, you farted on my face because of excitement?" or "Did you know that I bought your Christmas gift from a goodwill store? We were very poor then, but you were so proud to show it to your friends?" or "You look more handsome when you had your entire tooth removed." Recollecting and laughing over these funny memories is priceless. The loving experience of being with someone at old age makes life, though countable in years, worth living.

Old age being a few steps toward the graveyard is a reality that most old people fear to think about. When my father was bedridden, my mother cared for him with love and dedication and still had fun with her children and grandchildren. She knew one day my father would leave her, but she continued to shower him with love until his last days. It was only when she saw my father's coffin being lowered to the grave that she released a loud cry of losing him. Five years later, she joined him. They were married for sixty-six years.

Part II

Perversion and Addiction:
Frailties of Being Human

Under any given

set of environmental conditions

an experimental animal will behave

as it damn well pleases.

(Murphy's First Law of Biology)

Perversions and Addictions

I was shopping in the mall one Sunday with my daughter when I saw a young couple having fun. The guy tossed up the woman and caught her up the air with a hug and swung her around as he put her down. The two teenagers walking before us loudly commented, "Perverts," referring to the couple who were having fun. In another occasion while waiting for the go signal in an intersection, the couples inside the car before us hugged and kissed each other until the signal light changed; they were both female. My husband commented, "Perverts." Free will entitles anyone a limitless kind of behavior according to their likes; but for the sake of decorum, society puts some limitation to this freedom, sometimes imposing penalties or even punishments. But who would limit or prohibit a man from wearing a woman's underwear, or a woman wearing a man's brief, if that's how they like it? When does an act or behavior become a perversion? In whatever form or manner, no one really has the right to meddle in another person's exercise of his free will. Accordingly, what is perverse to the eyes of the observer may be normal to the person doing the act.

By street definition, "perversion" is any act that any observer finds abnormal, offensive, unnatural, and weird. To the academicians and those in the medical-therapy profession, perversion is a debatable subject to define. Different schools of thought had their own definition and opinion of the term, thus placing the issue on perversion unresolved. Even the classification of a pervert act into sexual and nonsexual is philosophically debated. Some group considered an act sexual when the intent is reproduction; other group labels an act as sexual as long as such act uses the sexual organs in the copulation that is without the intent to reproduce (Soble 2006, vol.II). In the past, morality and social acceptance were the bases for labeling sexual acts as perversions. Churches and religious organizations even viewed perversion as a sin. With society transforming, some acts that were considered pervert before are now normal in the eyes of others.

Humans possess the faculty to use reason to justify their action, but when it comes to sexual urges, some humans behave much less than the lower forms of animals. Lions don't have sex with tigers; elephants don't have sex with monkeys; cats don't have sex with dogs; but humans, some do have sex with animals (bestiality), with statues (Pygmalion's), with dead persons (necrophilia), and with any other objects that caused them the sexual urges (fetishism). These are real perversions because it defies nature, social norms, morality, and reasons. I recall a boy during my elementary days who was caught inserting his private part into a hole he made on the banana trunk, similar to the movie *American Pie.* He was trying to explore how it feels to insert an erect penis into a hole. Was it perversion? Should a young boy be called a pervert by doing this? Others would say yes; but others say he was not because at his particular age, he was not expected to insert his erect penis into a girl's vagina, being a minor and not yet ready for such act. He was just experimenting. In another instance a boy was rushed to the hospital because his penis got stuck to a rubber toy. He was aroused by some sexual thoughts, then he saw a rubber toy with a small hole; he inserted his erect penis but could not pull it out because the wall of the rubber toy created a vacuum when he inserted his penis. In like manner he could not be considered a pervert.

Masturbation back then was also considered a perversion. I remember while staying in my aunt's boardinghouse and feeling the heat inside a crowded room, the residents and I always spent our evening on the rooftop of the next apartment behind my aunt's. We passed through the bathroom window using a ladder, then came out on the roof of the next building. One night we saw through the window of the other building a guy who was flipping a magazine while he lay flat on his chest on his bed. Then he stood up and rubbed the magazine to the genital area of his body. He took off his clothes, looked at himself in the mirror, took the magazine, rubbed it again to his genitals, and masturbated. For weeks we saw him doing it again and again until one night he overheard some noise outside of his window. He looked around to investigate where the noise came from. Sensing it was coming from the rooftop directly visible from his window, he closed the windows.

I understood masturbation at an early age when I was made to type those pornographic materials of my boss. What scared me to do it was the forbidding words from my parents that if done regularly and without moderation would cause blindness, madness, diseases, and sudden death. Wouldn't it be a shame to be blind for the rest of your life or suddenly die just because of masturbation? The issue of becoming blind because of excessive masturbation was resolved when I asked a friend who was a sex therapist if that was true. He said some sex therapists would even recommend masturbation sometimes for health reasons. Biologically, the human body follows a monthly cycle of replenishing some body fluids for health reasons, like menstruation in women. Nature's ways of replenishing the male fluids such as the semen is through wet dreams. In their sleep they dream of having sex that when they woke up, their underpants were soaked with semen, discharged while they were asleep. In the absence of wet dreams, masturbation is recommended.

Another form of perversion is indecent exposure or exhibitionism. News of some men and women caught exhibiting their sex organs in public places occupies the newspaper, television, and the Internet. Some of them were even celebrities. Entertainers such as Madonna, Britney Spears, and Christina Aguilera have wild sexual and sensual interpretations in their music videos. It is their form of expressing how they view sex through their music. One of Michael Jackson's popular moves when performing before a large crowd was touching his crotch as he jerked. However, as these celebrities get older, their sexual exhibitionism gradually diminished, and a new group of exhibitionists takes over in the music world. Sexual exhibitionism is to them a way of being noticed by their adoring fans.

Homosexuality was also considered a perversion until Dr. Simon LeVay, a neurobiologist at the Salk Institute in La Jolla,

California, discovered in his research work that the cell clusters in the brain known as INAH3 varies in size between heterosexual and homosexual men, the latter's being in the same size range as women's, therefore concluding that homosexuality is then genetic. On the other hand, homosexuality, the attraction to a person with the same sex, is considered contrary to natural law; they are intrinsically a disordered relationship (Rice, 1999). But now that the issue of homosexuality gains acceptance under normal standards, so many have come out from their closets and are demanding equal treatment in the eyes of the law, particularly the laws of marriages both in the civil courts and the church's.

Men called "Casanovas," who finds pleasure in seducing women, are considered sex addicts in some aspects. Believing themselves as a dominant male, they obsess to deflower or impregnate every girl as many as possible. He could be married or unmarried, but this does not matter to him because his intention is only to have pleasure in seducing women. Psychologists viewed the behavior of Casanovas as one whose sex appetite is like that of eating food—like *eating* the woman he seduces. It was noted though that this kind of addiction diminishes as the person aged (Crime and Punishment: The Illustrated Crime Encyclopedia, 4:497). I know of a man who was like this; he gets excited by every woman he gets near to and would find ways to have sex with that woman. The mere sight of a woman's breasts or legs and thighs aroused him. It did not matter to him if the female object is ugly, old, or fat. One person who knew about him even commented that "anything, as long as it wears a skirt, aroused him." He added that if the lamppost wears a skirt, he would have sex with it.

On the female version, they are the "nymphomaniacs" who use their body to seduce men in order to gain influence, power, and control. They are sometimes called "man eaters," like Delilah, a biblical woman who caused Samson's weakness when she cut his hair. Messalina, the wife of the Roman emperor Claudius; Julia, the daughter of Augustus Caesar; Lola Montes, Isabela Duncan, Marie Tarnowsky, among others, are women noted for using their body and their beauty to control powerful men (Crime and Punishment: The Illustrated Crime Encyclopedia, 10:1241). We had a neighbor who was said to be a nymphomaniac. The parents noticed her sickness when she was still nine years old. She was always seen rubbing her vagina to a post or to any hard object she could find. During her teenage days, she could be seen being surrounded by boys of her age taking turns in having sex with her. Sometimes she would give money to the boys just to have sex with her. When her parents learned of her activities, they imprisoned her in her room or tied her whenever she felt the urge. She was institutionalized until she died.

Other forms of perversions include oral sex (fellatio and cunnilingus), anal sex (sodomy), voyeurism (sexual gratification through looking at sexual acts or objects), exhibitionism (sexual gratification by public exposure of one's body or genitals), and transvestitism (mostly male dressing up and acting like a female to attract male clients). Some perversions are considered criminal, like pedophilia (sexual gratification preferably with children), sadism (sexual gratification obtained through the infliction of pain upon others), masochism (a condition in which sexual gratification depends on being dominated, cruelly treated, beaten, etc.), and incest (having sexual relationship with a family member).

Couples, even married ones, sometimes make love in a pervert manner. They do sex inside the elevator, on top of a kitchen table, on the couch, in the bathtub, at the porch, inside the closet, in the restroom, at the movie houses, and everywhere. An array of "how to" books are sold in bookstores, teaching couples how to enjoy sex in many different ways. Most of them fall under the street definition of the word "perversion." Doing sex depends on the values of each couple. Wild couples do it wildly, while conservative couples do it conservatively. Views and opinions about sexual behavior of couples depend on who is viewing it; wild couples viewing the performances of the conservative couples finds them boring; while conservative couple, looking at the performances of the wild couples, look at them as savages or perverts.

Any sexual behavior that is addictive, compulsive, and uncontrollable has to be referred to a psychiatrist; or it would turn to sexual insanity. We can see a number of celebrities confessing in television interviews their addiction to sex and how it ruins their lives; others hide their shame in drugs and alcohol. The remedy recommended for this kind of behavior was institutional rehabilitation. Most recently, Tiger Woods joined the club of sexually addicted celebrities. Individuals doing pervert acts are known to be of aloof personality, antisocial, and shy; others are the opposite. They do pervert acts for show and attention getting.

Prostitution

The entire block across the place where my parents run a boardinghouse and a dress-shop business was known as the red-light district. Across the west side of the block was an old university established during the Spanish era, and across the south side was the back door entrance of another university, which had the biggest student population in the region. On the perimeter, except the south side, were businesses of all sorts; and inside the block were houses mostly doing prostitution as business. The entire neighborhood was a busy hub mostly lodging-boardinghouse businesses, and students commuted to and from school every day except Sundays. The residents inside the red-light district could access all sides of the block, but they used the south side because the street lighting was poor — the right place for them to conceal their identity and a good waiting place for pimps. This was the only strip not used by the students on their way to their respective boardinghouses. They would have to turn around the lighted commercial streets to get to their places. Our place was on the south side behind a university, along the back door entrance.

We were the first to open a commercial establishment on the south side that stayed open up to ten o'clock in the evening. The pimps would intimidate us by standing nearby and by scaring away our customers. In response to their intimidation, my brother and his buddies, who were constables, spent time singing and drinking in front of our establishment until whenever they like to leave, thus obstructing their business. Gradually new businesses followed suit until the whole strip became alive and well lighted. It was then that students began using the street when they go to and from school. The pimps would only come out when all the business establishments were closed at night.

My parents' business was doing well because of the presence of the students in the area. After doing my schoolwork, I helped my parents sew clothes for their customers, and most of them I knew by their faces. One evening while I was looking through the window around past midnight, I saw girls coming out from the red-light district wearing the clothes that I made. There were three of them escorted by a pimp. They hailed a taxi, and the girls went inside, leaving the pimp behind. I could not believe what I saw. I knew these girls were college students. Intrigued about their secret lives, I watched them through the window every night as they took a taxi. At daybreak when I woke up, I saw them got out from a taxi and then back to the houses inside the block.

When they come to my mother's dress shop, I initiated to befriend them with small talks. The three of them did not hesitate to open up in casual conversation their secret lives. "Why do you have to go out every night?" was my first question. I learned from their answer that the fee was better if they go to the man's place, mostly a hotel or on the beach. There they would have two or more men at one time, which earned them a bigger take-home service fee because each of the men would pay separately. I asked why and where on the beach. They didn't give me an answer. When I asked my male friends the same question, their answer was intriguing. They prefer to have sex on the beach with the lower half of the bodies submerged in sea water. After the sex act, they dip their bodies into the sea. It was their belief that the germs of sexually transmitted diseases die in salty water; therefore, they could not get the disease. I wondered why these girls were so candid and open about their profession as prostitutes. I was anticipating that they would shy away from my intrusion to their private lives, but to my surprise they were very cooperative.

The casual talk, while they wait for their dresses, was matter-of-factly. I asked how many were the maximum number of customers they had in a day. Was there an instance when they got attracted to a particular customer? Did they ever have a feeling of satisfaction in every encounter they had? In a manner of somewhat being amused and shy, the answer was, "It depends." It depends on the kind of customer they had. For the amateurs, those who were first timers in sex, they do most of the manipulation, teaching the neophyte how to do it; those who were in a hurry as if afraid of something, they need not take their clothes; those who were like animals on the loose, wild and hot, they just let them do whatever they wanted to do; and those who were regular and experienced, they established repeat contact. The last type was where they could sometimes develop love and affection. There were also those who came, only to change their minds and leave without having sex. "How about sadist and violent men, do you experience them too?" I asked. They gave an affirmative answer. Some men inflict physical pain on them, sometimes using foreign objects into their vagina. I did not ask further.

Transvestites were no strangers in my parents' dress shop. They frequented the place for two reasons. One, to have their clothes done specific to their own designs; and two, they were looking for male prospects in my parents' boardinghouse because we had a number of them on the third floor. They would lure the boys with cash and other things, such as clothes and perfumes, in exchange for sex. I remember one of the transvestites had a crush on my boyfriend, but when he learned I was the girlfriend, he stopped. When my father learned about their intentions, he reprimanded them not to victimize our male lodgers or else they could not come to our place anymore. Some of them went to our place to do home-service manicure and pedicure, as well as haircuts to our lodgers. A transvestite friend was even the one who did my makeup and hairdo during my wedding.

One day a young pretty lady applied for a bed space in our lodging house. She was a college student enrolled at the university behind our building. She said she came from the province and needed a place to stay while studying in the city. She was lucky to get a bed space that day. The first few months of her stay were just ordinary. She went to work at daytime and to school at nighttime. Then we noticed there were nights she would not go to school but instead waited for a private car to pick her up and would come home at daybreak. I did not hesitate to confront her of her latest activity. She confided that she was running short of money and would probably quit studying. Here she told me the circumstances of her life. When she was in her first year of college, she met a young guy who impregnated her, thus forcing her to stop schooling. Afraid that her parents would let her go home to the province, she begged the guy to marry her. The guy was a son of a local politician. The sad part about it was that the mother of the guy did not approve of her becoming a daughter-in-law. She allowed her to stay with them until the delivery of the baby, after which she was given a large sum of money to leave. She used the money to go back to school.

When she could not meet her expenses anymore, she asked assistance from a friend of the politician's son. She was picked up by the guy that night and was brought to a private room in a hotel. Inside was a gathering of men who just concluded their political conference. She could not turn back; she needed the money very badly. She was made to walk naked on top of the conference table while the men reached out to touch her body with lust in their eyes. From that time on, every guy in that group would pick her up from the lodging house and check her in the hotel for a paid sex. When my sister learned about this, she kicked her out from our place to protect the image of the other female residents. Two years after, I heard she got married but died during the delivery of her baby.

I was invited one time by my cousin to a welcome party for the boss of her husband who was visiting their local office. At the reception, I noticed two young pretty ladies seated beside the guest. I thought at first that these ladies were the guest's daughters because they were so young and innocent looking. I was told later those were local prostitutes who would service him for the evening at the hotel where he was staying. Every time the boss comes around, he always asked two, not one, women to make his night pleasurable. I learned it was common practice in every government office that when a top executive visits a local office, part of the reception is a woman, a prostitute, to service his sexual needs for the night in a hotel.

In another instance a close friend invited me to an exclusive club where wives of politicians and executives hanged around at night. A dance instructor entertained the women; in return, they slid in his pocket a fee for dancing with her. If she wanted sex, they could check in upstairs, the club being part of the hotel building. On the other side of the building was a male-striptease club with mostly women as customers, sometimes gay guys.

Women inside the club could go wild, like reaching to touch the male sex organ to be aroused. Once aroused she could request for a male partner and a room space upstairs. The building and the clubs were owned by a local politician.

One time late after midnight, my roommates and I went out to buy food. Since we knew there were vendors on the street along the movie houses downtown, we went there. As we strolled along the sidewalks, we saw young muscular good-looking men waiting to be picked up by some sex-hungry women—mostly old, rich, and widowed. Their service fees depend on how long the woman wanted the guy to stay. The place could either be in her house or in a hotel. We always think that men are the only pleasure seekers who would spend their money for sex—women, too. It is reported that a number of women regularly visits pornographic sites in the Internet.

A young girl whose face is covered with heavy makeup and dressed seductively showing cleavage was always presumed to be a prostitute. This assumption originated from the concept that to attract a male for sex, a girl has to look pretty and seductive. Being brought up by a conservative family, I also tend to believe this presumption as true; I have never seen a prostitute who doesn't cover her face with makeup and wear seductive clothes. To discourage my female students from wearing facial makeup at an early age, I made up the story about King Solomon, linking cosmetics to prostitution. I told them that during the time of King Solomon, women competed with each other in who among them would King Solomon choose to have sex with at night. The woman he chose would be rewarded with clothing, food for her household, jewelries, money, and expensive perfume—a practice descriptive of prostitution. In the hopes of getting the reward again, the woman whom King Solomon had sex the previous night, having been used and bruised by the king, would conceal her dry skin and sunken eyes with cosmetics and perfume so the king could not recognize her as the woman he had sex the night before. After telling the story, the male students in my class would tease the girls wearing makeup by asking them, "What did you do last night?" It was like insinuating that the girls were covering their faces with cosmetics to conceal marks and bruises from sexual activities.

Prostitution was a way of life for women during the olden times. In ancient Greece and Rome, "sacred" prostitution flourished in many temples. Women stayed in the temples, waiting for men to give them coins for sex. They sit in the temple and give themselves to any man who threw silver coins on their laps. They offered their body as a duty to their deity, after which they were discharged and could go home. Pretty women got home early, but the ugly ones had to stay until she fulfilled the conditions, which the law demanded. Some women mostly the ugly ones stayed as much as three or four years (Liberated Christians. 1997). Prostitution was said to be the oldest profession ever since the Bible days. In the olden times, women could not make a living because they did not have education. Their roles were to serve a husband and to take care of the children. When a man divorced her, she would be left with the children and without money. Because of this, some women sold their bodies for money in order to live. Prostitution existed during this time because the laws on marriage were strict and stern. Only men of abundant resources can marry and have several wives; he can decide when to keep or kick out a wife. Men who cannot afford content themselves with prostitutes, usually the women that was kicked out or divorced and without money.

The business of prostitution penetrates all levels of society—from the rich and famous down to the slum area. Innocent women are lured with a promise of a decent job in the city, only to end up in places where there is no escaping. The operators would lavish the girls with clothes, jewelries, perfumes, and money allowances, a way of putting them in debts. Some girls managed to escape, while others were unfortunate. To survive, they just have to accept their fate. In the process they learned to accept it and become expert in the trade.

Prostitution also invaded the world of innocent children. In 1885 child prostitution was legal in London. Young girls were the preference of the male clientele. The younger the girl, the more they pay for the service because sexual pleasure was the best in a girl with a tight vagina. Mothers were even involved in this trade. They gave their young girls to prostitution in exchange for money. It took a newspaper editor named William Thomas Stead to campaign against it and change the law but, ironically, landed him in jail. He was one of those who perished with the

Titanic in 1912 (Crimes and Punishments: The Illustrated Crime Encyclopedia, 5:579-585). In most Muslim countries like Pakistan, Afghanistan, and Iran, child prostitution is a booming business because younger or older men search for girl with tight vagina, which only young girls ranging from ages nine to seventeen can provide. In some parts of the world, parents sold their children to prostitution because of extreme economic hardship. Young boys with inflamed genitals caused by some pedophiles have been on the record, and parents just kept it secret from authorities because of shame and fear that the authorities might punish them. During my days, or even before that, there were isolated reports of sexual crimes committed against children by adults; but the perpetrator just got away from it because there was no law to protect the rights of these children. Children were told by the predators not to report his crime or he would kill him and his parents.

Now various support groups are formed to help and protect the rights of women and children. To give awareness on the evils of prostitution and the wide spread of sexually transmitted diseases is the main focus of these groups. They also fight for legislation, protection, and education needed to eradicate the business of prostitution. In spite of all this effort, being the oldest of all profession, prostitution stays.

Pornography

I was seventeen years old when pornography was first introduced indirectly to me in the early '60s. During that time, circulation of pornographic materials was clandestine and limited to circles of friends only. My boss, who I thought was in his mid-forties at that time, always asked me to make copies of the pornographic materials he got, which he also distributed to his friends and associates. That experience faded from my memories as I moved on to my priorities in life, which was to finish college, to get a job, and to settle down in marriage when I meet the right man. Later in my adult life, already married, I ask some of my male friends and relatives, among them my nephews, son, and husband which pornographic materials they prefer the most that give them more erotic response. To them printed materials excite the imagination and has prolonged enjoyment over visual pornography. Reading printed pornography excites the imagination in a slow motion, awaiting one scenario after another, and the level of bodily discomfort gradually heightens until the final release. In visual pornography, the excitement is instant upon viewing the actual performances. The enjoyment is for a short time only. It is for this reason that the viewer does it over and over until addiction sets in.

In the office where I worked, the male employees would beg the female employees not to do overtime whenever someone brought a copy of pornographic materials. They would stay behind and view the pictorial materials together or read aloud the texts to arouse everyone. We could tell their excitement over the experience because the next day they still talked about it, forgetting there were women who sometimes overheard them.

When Betamax, a video player, came out, the one that got the video also brought with him the video player. Adult movies for public viewing were also rare. Most of the adult movies were strictly censored, and if they were released for public viewing, some obscene scenes were already removed. One time when the movie *40 Carats* was released, four of my classmates wanted to see it. We requested a male friend to get us a ticket because everyone in the line was male. Only the five of us seated in one row were female; the rest were all male. We tried to talk in whispers, but still our voices were very distinctive to the guys near us, so they moved away from us. We couldn't help but giggle about the experience. Even in the school campus, we prided talking about the movie to our female friends.

In the university where I was studying, a separate section of the library was restricted for access. Sex books and others that the priests educators considered morally offensive to students were kept in this section. Some books have a lot of missing pages because male students, mostly medical students, when given admission to the restricted section, tore down the pages with drawings of the female sex organ and pictures of sexual intercourse.

Now pornography invades the Internet that access becomes easy even to children. Typing the word "pornography" or "sex" in the search engine of the Internet does not take one to pornographic Web sites at once. There is a long list of Web sites to select from; some of them are informative articles for and against pornography. One doesn't need a credit card to have a view of pornographic materials in the Internet. There are sites that are free to view, and one can have his pick. Once a site is opened, one will find a grid showing the different names and faces of women. Pointing the mouse to the picture will tell what that particular woman does in the video. Clicking it would open the video for the viewer to see. These are just sample performances, but the mere sight of these videos is enough to arouse the viewer. To access a long presentation, one has to sign in for membership and make available his credit card for charges.

Web sites on child pornography are dangerous zones to visit since these are monitored sites. These are criminal acts, and regular visitors are tapped by the authorities because only child molesters and predators frequent these pages. In same-sex pages, all that a visitor can find are performances on oral and anal sex. For a heterosexual viewer, visiting these pages is just a matter of curiosity. The first time I saw a same-sex performance was years ago when I accidentally saw my boyfriend, who was gay, having sex with his "cousin" in his apartment. Back then in the seventies, it was difficult to recognize a homosexual. They cover their acts by having a girlfriend.

Pornography really did not affect my attitude about sex. Ever since the time I first got hold of pornographic materials, I understood why men are drawn to this. My husband did not know I visit pornographic Web sites every some times when he is asleep. It really intrigues me to see and to find how I would react, comparing this experience to what I had when I was typing pornographic texts. I want to see and feel the experience of viewing a pictorial pornography (for the purpose of this book). I look at every detail of the body movements, the moaning sound, the facial expression, and the passionate aspect of their performance. What I first notice is most of the performances begin with oral sex. Women are seen kneeling down or bending as they perform oral sex. They seem to enjoy their role as a sex-hungry person, using their mouth as if eating the male organ with gusto. It is obvious why oral sex is mostly emphasized—because most of the viewers are male—and all men love fellatio. Even married men would ask their wives to perform oral sex sometimes. In group sex, a single woman is penetrated in her anus and in her vagina while she performs oral sex to the third man—a sight that is only for show, as you will see how uneasy that was to all the parties involved in the act. In all the performances that I viewed, I didn't see a real orgasm happening; if there was, that could be faked with a gasping sound from both parties. In real orgasm, both the male body and the female body quiver and stiffen as if suspended and frozen as the sex fluids are being released. When orgasm happens, one can see both partners tensely and tightly hugging each other's body like they don't want to let go of each other. If the cameraman captures this moment closely with his lens, the viewer will see the sex organs tensed as if like throbbing.

Swingers, exhibitionists, and wife swappers also videotape their activities and post their performances to the pornography sites in the Internet. A number of them are celebrities who find sex as a way of making them more popular. Others are professionals, educated, and holding positions in big companies but hide their identities with wigs and makeup. It is their way of fighting boredom and stress in the office work. Their performances are surely real, not faked, but they are obviously depicting more of their value system than their performances, and perhaps trying to convince couple viewers to be like them. Even though they are real couples doing sex, the presence of a cameraman make them conscious of their performances, thus not passionate enough to express real sex as an expression of love. We can tell that from the sound they make as they make love. In a very passionate lovemaking, neither of the couple makes loud sound because they are more focus on their effort to please the other. We can see the distinction in movies of lovemaking depicted by Hollywood. A loving, passionate expression of love through sexual intercourse is depicted as holistic, serene, tender, and devotional to the other partner. The animal version of this kind of lovemaking is that of the penguins. A sexual encounter that is full of animalistic passion is depicted with loud moaning sounds or even screaming and scratching each other as their bodies roll everywhere on the bed, sometimes falling down to the floor. It is as if each one partner is attacking or controlling the other or like having a fight. A male and female lions having sex are examples of this kind of lovemaking.

In the words of Pope John Paul II (*Reasons for Hope,* 1995), pornography is immoral and very much antisocial because it contradicts human veracity, with man being created in the image and likeness of God. Its proliferation is an indication of a broader decay of societies' moral values. Imagine two human beings doing sex in the Internet while millions of eyes are watching with erotic pleasure. Could we find in those two individuals the image of God? Human sexuality is a gift from God intended to open individuals to love and to share in his creative work through responsible procreation. The female body is not an object of lust but a partner in the creative process in the propagation of the species. Society will have to deal with the ills of pornography because it is impossible to eradicate this menace; it has even become a multibillion-dollar business with the advent of the Internet. As long as man craves for sexual gratification, pornography stays and prospers.

Pornography addiction has ruined many a marriage. Some husbands sleep very late at night to spend time and money viewing pornography. A couple friends we knew divorced because of this. His wife complained about his deficit spending, always borrowing money from her. When she found out his money was spent to credit charges on pornography, she turned down his loan requests. Another wife from among my friends complained about her husband performing on her what he saw at the pornography web sites he visited. She said he performed sodomy to her, and she hated it. Because of this, arguments and fights became regular in their household. We tried to help them save their marriage but to no avail, eventually, they divorced. Husbands with secret activities in the internet visiting pornography sites are putting themselves in big trouble. The compulsion to enjoy in actuality what was seen in the internet drives a husband to seek a partner, and it is always the wife that becomes the object. Others find outside relief but this could drain his finances as well. Another husband I know holding a prestigious teaching position in a university was caught by her daughter having cybersex using his webcam. He was seen masturbating before the webcam as he looks at the picture on the monitor of the bare breast of the woman on the other computer from somewhere. Other activities on the webcam go as far as exposing on camera their genitals as they imagine having actual sex with each other.

The actual loser in this pornography business is the viewer. Regular viewing drains out not only his finances but also his emotions for, although he got satisfaction in viewing them, he misses one vital part in his enjoyment of his sexuality — which is a partner. Sexual intercourse is not a solo performance. One must have a partner to share with the ecstasy and the pleasure sex brings. Once the emotional side of the viewer is eroded with guilt and degradation, anger and violence set in. Some men, who regularly view pornography to the point of addiction, become sex offenders or rapist. Crime is one of the fruits of pornography. Ted Bundy, the notorious serial killer, confessed pornography caused him to rape and kill his victims. Rapists, serial killers, and pedophiles spend most of their time viewing pornography before looking for a victim (Crimes and Punishments: The Illustrated Crime Encyclopedia, 1:35-56). How many decent men have been caught with their secret lives of pornography and became a news topic on TVs and magazines: a model schoolteacher hooking a camera in the ladies' restroom and viewing what the girls were doing in the rest room on the monitor under his classroom table; a university president caught keeping a list of telephone numbers of the young girls living in the dormitories and calling these numbers for erotic and sexual messages; a senator, a congressman, a businessman, and the lists go on. Another close friend told us that his friend who is a priest always goes to his house with pornographic videos to view, because he could not view this in the convent. This priest is said to have children with one woman known to some of his parishioners.

Pornography uses a variety of media, ranging from animation, drawing, film, painting, printed literature, photos, sculpture, sound recording, video, to video games. Legal treatment of pornography varies widely from country to country. Most countries consider soft-core pornography less offensive and could be shown on TV or sold in general stores. On the other hand, hard-core pornography is regulated and limited in distribution. Child pornography and those that depict violence or perverse sex with other objects, such as animals or dead person, are strictly restricted; and a penalty is imposed if someone is found in distribution of or showing and viewing them. Conservatives and liberals, feminists, as well as religious groups, continue to disagree with each other over almost all aspects of pornography—from exclusions and inclusions in its definition, from rights in free expression to rights in privacy, of censorship, and legality; while the pornographers, on the other hand, continue to expand their operation in all parts of the world. It has become a multibillion-dollar industry and still expanding worldwide with the availability of the Internet, cell phones, and other electronically operated image gadgets. We can only sigh what kind of society awaits us in the future if pornography becomes like daily bread for every person, young and old.

Sex and Crime

I was alone at the backyard of our house playing with our new puppies when an older guy dragged me to a corner behind the door of a vacant building adjacent to our house. At age five, I had no idea what he was about to do; but thanks to my father who was then looking for me because it was almost sunset, I was spared from his evil intentions. After that incident, my family moved to the city. Ten years later, I learned that the guy was sentenced for life without parole for killing a prime witness to the crime he and his friends committed in the neighborhood. In the place where I grew up, sex crime against children was remote and isolated; or if there was, the community had no knowledge about it, or maybe the aggrieved parties were just ashamed to make it public.

In the early fifties, the Honorable John Rossetti, judge of Stark County Common Pleas Court, Canton, Ohio, and former assistant attorney general of Ohio, worked hard to reduce sex crimes in Ohio for many years. After eleven years of legal battle, appearing six times before the Ohio legislature, a bill requiring the registration of convicted sex offenders was finally enacted into law. Since then the Habitual Sex Offenders Law, which became effective on October 4, 1963, had set the pattern all over the United States. After the brutal murder of a 13-year-old girl whose ravished body was found in a gravel pit, William L. Lombard, Chief of Police Rochester, New York set up the "Moral Squad" to control and contain sexual crimes in 1962 (Crimes and Punishments: The Illustrated Crime Encyclopedia, 18:2131-2134). Crime against the innocent has been around since the beginning of time, but people just did not give so much attention to this until it finally hit their homes. Parents, who were victims of losing their child, with the support of the community and the law enforcers, organized in 1996 the "Amber Alert" — named after the little girl Amber Hagerman who was abducted without a trace. Whenever a child is reported missing, the "Amber Alert" is activated in all media facilities, like billboards, newspapers, radios, televisions, and the Internet, to make everyone aware and be involved in finding the missing child. Megan's Law, named after Megan Kanka of New Jersey, is another federal law passed in 1996 that authorizes agencies to notify the public about convicted sex offenders living, working, or visiting their community. Megan Kanka was a seven-year-old girl who was raped and killed by a known child molester who moved across the street from the family. Sex offenders are living everywhere in America. These are individuals who look ordinary in the neighborhood until news of abduction and rape happens.

Crimes committed involving sex occupies a regular space in newspapers, television, and the Internet. Few of the cases in the twenty-eight (28) volumes of *Crimes and Punishments:The Illustrated Crime Encyclopedia* are worth mentioning here. A case in point is that of Mary Flora Bell of Scotswood, England. She was only eleven years old in 1968 when she strangled a four-year-old neighbor (2:239-246). Mary Bell's background indicated child abuse and rejection by her mother after birth. She was an illegitimate child of an emotionally disturbed mother. Sexual and physical abuses during childhood made young boys kill at a very young age like Peter Kurten, among others. He confessed to have orgasm when he killed his victims (14:1644-1649).

Psychotherapists, psychologists, psychoanalysts, and other related medical practitioners could give us a list of causes that drove young children and adults to commit heinous crimes involving sex. Dr. Dorothy Otnow Lewis, author of *Guilty by Reason of Insanity*, made an investigative research on what causes young inmates in prison to kill at an early age. She discovered after a thorough evaluation on her subjects that two of the factors that lead these killers to do vicious crimes were poverty and sexual abuses inflicted on them during their childhood by some adults. Emotional stress and helplessness during the sexual assaults at a young age were too heavy to handle for a child's brain causing it to snap and became neurotic and violent. Some even developed multiple personalities. In this book, Dr. Lewis and her colleague, the eminent neurologist Jonathan Pincus, searched to understand the origins of violence and how our justice system treated the crimes committed by these killers and the kind of punishment imposed upon them. Places like orphanages and troubled homes produce individuals wanting of love; they tend to be angry, antisocial, hateful, neurotic, psychotic, and shy. Emotional and physical traumas caused by sexual abuses, rejection experienced with parents, siblings, classmates, friends and relatives, unrequited love, mental illness, and hereditary criminal instincts are among the listed causes of their violent behavior. Most of them view pornographic materials before committing their crimes. Other vicious criminals show hatred of the opposite sex that they enjoy seeing their victims suffer by burning or torturing them alive, and mutilating or eating their flesh. In Shirley Lynn Scott's *What Makes Serial Killers Tick, 1999,* a detailed discussion is made about possible causes why these different individuals become serial killers. She concluded that these killers live on the other side of our social boundaries. She considered them as human black holes. They feel something in them is missing that makes them feel like dead within, an unfathomable feeling of emptiness inside. Their victims are "a blank" as they don't care who that person is and what that person feels because they are also blank to themselves.

While most sex criminals are men, women also are reported to have committed sexual crimes. Tracy Wigginton, a committed lesbian, a devil worshipper, and an occultist coerced friends and followers to kill for her. She and her friends randomly picked up victims with a promise of sex, then kill the victim. Tracy, practicing occultism, drank the blood of their victim (13:1537-1541). Other women use their sexuality and wealth to control their lovers and to make them kill their husbands, like Alice Arden, Catherine Hayes, Cora Mckown, Florence Bravo, and Edith Thompson (13:1515-1519; 4:458-465). The passionate, pretty, and impulsive Alma Rattenbury, wanting of love and affection, which she could not get from an alcoholic husband (27:3234-3240), posted an ad for a male house helper aged fourteen to eighteen. A young seventeen-year-old guy responded to her ad, who later became her lover. She lavished him with love and material comfort, which made him more demanding, throwing tantrums. Insanely jealous, her lover hacked her husband to death.

Domestic violence, considered a sexual assault done by a husband to a wife, is also reported to be one of the rising problems authorities encounter every day. A number of wives, in some cases including the children, are reported missing, killed, and mutilated by their own husbands. Drugs, financial problems, infidelity, sex rejection, and deprivation are among the factors that cause marital relationship to be vicious and violent. There are husbands or wives who hire an assassin to kill the other for financial reason or just to get away from a troubled marriage. Jealousy, extreme dependence, and obsession of the other often drive a husband or wife to kill rather than lose the other partner.

Other sex-related offenses considered as criminal in nature are child molestation (pedophilia), child pornography, child prostitution, child rape, incest, and sadism. Persons engaged in these kinds of activities are viewed as antisocial, immature, and psychotic. Pedophiles are considered criminals wherever they live, including those engaged in child prostitution, child pornography, and child rape. Punishment could be death or life imprisonment without parole depending on the place the crime was committed. Because incest happens within the family confines, it is difficult for authorities to establish the charges because family members opted to keep it out of public concern. In sadistic crime, if the victim died of the torture and violence inflicted, the charges thus become murder. If the victim survives and he/she does not file a complain, the sadist just gets away from his crime.

It is sad to note that no matter how much we want to minimize sex-related crimes, we cannot eradicate the causes why these criminals become such. There are always parents, relatives, friends who bully, control, dominate, intimidate, neglect, or reject young children. All that these children want is the feeling of being loved and accepted unconditionally. Technology invaded every household all over the world and modern gadgets and toys replace hugs and care for our children. Both parents now leave their homes for work giving the care for their children to nurseries and nannies. These children grow up wanting of love and affection from their parents. Traumatic situations, including traumas in the nurseries unknown to the parents could cause young children to snap. If not corrected early, these children become confused, disoriented, deranged, or angry as they grow. They grow up with the trauma in their psyche and their only way of fighting back or expressing their pain is to victimize another in some ways similar to what they have experienced. The cycle of violence continues, and on the outskirt are innocent individuals, who hope for a brighter tomorrows, randomly become victims of their crimes.

Sexually Transmitted Diseases

When I was seven years old, I remember having a scuffle with a classmate who threw my pair of shoes over the fence to make me give up the swing I was using. He had moist yellowish smelly scabs all over his body, said to be the result of a father frequenting brothels. His father acquired a sexually transmitted disease called gonorrhea, which he passed on to this son during his wife's pregnancy. When I told my mother about the scuffle and why I had blood stains inside my fingernails and some in my clothes, she asked who the villain was. I told her it was my classmate, the son of our neighbor across the street. She heated up water and gave me a thorough cleaning, then put rubbing alcohol all over my body. At that time I never bothered to ask my mother why she bathed me that way and what gonorrhea was.

During my early childhood, I recalled a vagabond roaming in our neighborhood who was said to be infected with syphilis. Whenever he was around, children threw stones at him and would run away from him. I could still visualize how his body looked like because he went around naked and disoriented. All parts of his body were covered with moist brownish pimplelike blisters. Nobody would approach him or would go near him to give cover to his body. The clothes people offered were thrown from a distance toward him, but he never took any of those clothing to cover him. Maybe the clothes would only stick to his moist body and would be difficult to remove. Sometimes he could be seen like having a visual problem because he walked erratically, as if not knowing where he was going. Authorities could not find a single family member to keep him off the street. He was said to have come from another town. Some compassionate families regularly give him food to eat, but they never went near him. They would just leave the food in a plate then signaled him to get it and eat it. Water was also included in his regular ration. One night he was found dead among the garbage.

During my teenage days, my parents told us stories about how a person could get infected with sexually transmitted diseases. They would say we could get STDs, such as herpes, through kissing. To discourage us from dating with our boyfriends in the movie house, they would scare us by saying movie houses were possible places to get STDs. In darkness and without sunlight, the germs there were preserved, and who knew the previous occupant of the seats was a prostitute. They said some men who could not afford a hotel used the movie house to have sex with a prostitute or with a girlfriend and leave on the seats their fluids. We were also forbidden to use public or movie-house toilets and public swimming pools for the same reason. In my parents' dress shop, prostitutes regularly come to have their clothes made. After they left, my sister would wipe thoroughly with alcohol the vacated bench because nobody would sit on it for fear that they might contract the germs or the pubic lice the prostitute left behind. Talking about pubic lice or "crabs," a flattened slice of beef meat soaked overnight with salt and placed over the vagina so the lice would stick to the meat was said to be the remedy to cure or eradicate the infestation. All along I thought that was really true, but when I asked friends in the medical profession about it, they said that was just for mockery. But how did that story come about if no one ever did that actually? Those who are knowledgeable about STDs or STIs would probably be laughing over these myths and superstition.

In tribal places in third world countries, sexually transmitted diseases are common because their unusual sex practices are part of their religious rituals and beliefs. In places like this, we can make a long list of myths and superstition about how they view sex, family, and their gods. These groups of people are difficult to convince to trust modern medicine. They have their own beliefs about the illness and also have their own cures, a ritual performed by their local quack doctor or spiritual leaders. When someone gets sick with STDs, they never view these as contagious or serious diseases; it was just an ordinary illness or perhaps a curse from their gods. More often herbal medicine is commonly used as a cure or perform a dance offering asking for forgiveness from the gods that cursed the infected individual. In a worldwide survey conducted by the World Health Organization in 1999, 340 million new cases of syphilis, gonorrhea, Chlamydia, and trichomoniasis in men and women aged fifteen to forty-nine years are reported. The largest number of new infections came from the regions of South and Southeast Asia, followed by sub-Saharan Africa and Latin American and the Caribbean regions. The regions of sub-Saharan Africa reported the highest rate of new cases per one thousand populations (http://www. avert.org/stdstatisticsworldwide.htm).

When my sister-in-law had a surgery on her right knee to remove the pus that was accumulating inside her knee calf, she blamed this to her husband. She did not know that every time her husband was away from home as a travelling mechanic of an oil company, he would spend some time with prostitutes. Because of this, when my brother got sick with gonorrhea and was having high fever, she refused to take care of him. She would not clean his bed, change his clothes, and serve him food. Looking at my brother in miserable condition, I took care of him, bought him antibiotics and vitamins, until he was fully cured from the disease. My other brother who also spent his free time at night with women of loose lives got a venereal disease known as syphilis. He was lucky that the infection was still in its early stage. He was rushed to the hospital with high fever. It was said that individuals infected with syphilis cannot have children, but this was proven wrong with my brother. He has two healthy and smart children.

Some men have sex with prostitutes on the beach because it was their belief that salty water kills the germs of the STDs; therefore, they don't get contracted with the disease. After having sex with the prostitute, they would dip in the sea to wash out the germs. This perhaps explained why a rich and promiscuous businessman and his bodyguards from our town always used girls on the beach at night. He and his bodyguards had the reputation of being sadist. Sometimes we heard talks that they would leave the prostitutes naked on the beach till morning, as they purposely hid their clothing. Onlookers and peeping Toms would inform his wife what he and his men did to the girls. She always brought clothes for the girls to wear and also gave money to let them go home. It was rumored the businessman died of a venereal disease.

Sexually transmitted diseases have broken so many families and have taken lives as well, but even with this fearful reality, men still continues to visit bawdy houses for sexual pleasures. I asked my two brothers what compelled them to seek this kind of pleasure. The plain answer that I got was that it is natural for men to seek pleasure with women. In the absence of a wife, prostitutes were next in their choices. Having sex with a girlfriend could possibly make her pregnant and, thus, becomes a big problem; prostitutes don't get pregnant. They said that the pimp always assured them and all other prospective customers that the girls were clean, regularly checked by a licensed doctor. Prostitutes are known to be carriers of STDs, yet in spite of the findings, men still visit brothels.

When AIDS (acquired immunodeficiency syndrome) was first discovered, it was thought that only homosexuals are infected with the disease and, in the process, become carriers of the disease once infected; but now heterosexuals are found to be infected as well. I have had friends and relatives who were homosexuals and have died, but I never had an idea what caused their death. Death of a homosexual infected with AIDS is a guarded secret by the relatives because they consider this as shameful. Some families disowned a homosexual family member and prefer not to be informed about their deaths. Except HIV and AIDS, sexually transmitted diseases such as bacterial vaginosis, Chlamydia, genital herpes, gonorrhea, syphilis, human papillomavirus, and trichomoniasis can be treated and cured easily and cheaply if diagnosed early enough. It is only when they are left untreated that their consequences are vital and could cause death.

People nowadays are well informed about STDs and AIDS, their causes, characteristics, symptoms, and cure. Charitable organizations and the World Health Organization work hand in hand in their eradication or at least to find a cure for these kinds of diseases. These organizations are finding ways to expand access to testing and treatment facilities and educate people about safer sexual practices and risk reduction. Sexually transmitted diseases are a major worldwide cause of acute illness, death, infertility, and long-term disability. Severe medical and psychological consequences for millions of men, women, and children are reported globally. STDs or STIs (sexually transmitted infections) and their complications are among the highest reasons for which adults seek medical help. STDs, excluding HIV, rank second to maternal factors as causes of diseases, death, and healthy life lost in women of childbearing age. Whatever kind of diseases or illnesses we acquired, some of us thinks of it as a punishment from God, that we did something wrong that made God punish us for it. We never think that we did something wrong to ourselves that made us sick. It is nature's law that overindulgence and abuses always have consequences. Having a misguided passion with a partner that is a carrier of the STD germs has irreversible and sometimes has fatal consequences.

Part III

*Anthropology: Who We
Are As Human Beings*

Man is an animal which,

among the animals,

refuses to be satisfied

by the fulfillment of animal desires.

—Alexander Graham Bell,

Sex Culture, Practices, and Rituals

As a child growing up, I thought of circumcision as nothing but a rite of passage for young boys into manhood. I witnessed how my four brothers and the neighborhood boys looked forward to this moment. It made them feel they were being transformed into a virile male confident of becoming a father one day. The process was rather crude, performed by a trusted old man in the neighborhood compared to one performed in the hospital by a doctor. Without anesthetics, a sharp knife was inserted into the penis with the blade facing the foreskin. A quick blow over the foreskin was then made, cutting the skin. The flow of blood was suppressed with a juice from guava leaves as an antiseptic. Then the boys were instructed to take a dip in the sea so healing would be effected and fast. There were reports of infections and sometimes hospitalization, but the situation was never life threatening. Later in my curious inquiry, because this practice really intrigued me, I learned it had its origin in the biblical times with the Jewish people. As what Jack Miles wrote in his book *God: A Biography* (1995), God demanded that Abram's penis—and the penises of all his descendants—be the symbol of Abram's covenant with God, that his fertility and the fertility of all his generations were not their own to exercise without divine participation. This practice had been followed by the Catholic Church in the sense that Christianity also used the Old Testament of the Jewish people in her teaching. Modern science rationalized that circumcision is practical for hygienic reasons since the foreskin is where sediments of dried semen stays and causes irritations and foul smell. However, in a circumcised male, the tip of the penis being partially exposed makes it very sensitive and could trigger sexual arousal. During those days, I could see how the neighborhood boys and my brothers prided over their circumcision as if it were a treasure. Young boys began wearing long pants, a show signifying their transformation into manhood, and at this stage, some of them started courting girls; you could see them following girls like little ants attracted to some sweet stuff. Young girls during our time were also subject to a rite of passage when we had our first menstruation—we were made to jump three steps from the stairs so that when we get married and become pregnant, we would not have a miscarriage during the first three months of pregnancy. When I had my first menstruation, I was so scared because I thought I could get pregnant if some boys would rape me or if I bathed in the swimming pool with the boys. Another common belief among the teenage boys had something to do with their acnes or pimples. The bloodstained panty of a girl menstruating for the first time was supposed to shrink the pimples and acnes. It always happened during the time when bloodstained panties of girls having their first menstruation were bleached under the sun; young boys would surely steal these panties for that purpose.

In ancient Egypt, reproduction and fertility were at the top of their social agenda. During this time Egyptians likely died young at childbirth, either the mother or the child, or both. Among those children who survived childbirth, about half died before their first birthday. Because of this, young girls left their household soon after their first menstruation to join in a ceremonial offering of fertility to Hathor, the fertility goddess. They left their household travelling with musicians/dancers/singers that went from one town to another for local festivities. In the festivity of dances, food, songs, and wine, the girls entertained the boys/men with their erotic dances and songs. Already in the state of being drunk and aroused, each pair culminated the festivities in a sexual intercourse. This was an opportunity for girls to become pregnant and bore a child. The girls who passed the test of giving birth and survived were highly priced for marriage. Where boys were initiated to adulthood in hunting and in war; girls likewise had to pass their initiation by bearing one or two children, as both initiations were considered a life-and-death situation (http://www.horemheb.com/sexuality.html).

Pederasty, an erotic relationship between an older man and an adolescent boy outside his immediate family, was a common practice in ancient Greece. It was seen as an educational institution for training young boys some cultural values, skills, and ethics, including sexual expression. It was like a coming-of-age rituals for young boys under the tutorials of the older men in the acquisition of virility, education, ethics, and military skills. Other places such as Japan, Korea, Central and North America, Russia, and some places in Europe had their own version of this practice. When the young boy reached a certain developmental levels and skills, he then in turn picked an adolescent boy and became his mentor. There had been controversies and issues with regard to this practice, even declaring it as illegal. It was viewed as a homosexual relationship as it involved sodomy or a case of pedophilia, being a sexual relationship between an older man and a younger boy (http://en.wikipedia.org/wiki/Pederasty).

The word "Kama Sutra" sounds like a blend of exotic and erotic ritual that promises a new experience for those who are seeking sexual fulfillment. Kama Sutra, a Hindu compilation of works of the Maurya period, is not a pornographic work. It is merely a systematic and impartial study of the essential aspects of being from courtship to sexual intercourse. It is the art of living for civilized and refined citizens, completing in the sphere of love, eroticism, and the pleasure of life. In Kama Sutra, eroticism—a perception of the divine state, is infinite delight. Kama Sutra is very much different compared to the Western interpretation in their pornographic videos. The book classifies the sexual organs of the males as a horse, which is the largest in size as in circumference and length; a bull, which is the medium size; and a hare, the small size. The female sex organs are the elephant, which has a wide opening; the hind, with medium opening; and the mare, with small opening. Proper matching of the sexual organs gives the partners ease in penetration and full excitement in copulation. If and when the sex organs are not matched, the book suggests techniques on how to fix the mismatch in order to have ease in penetration and full excitement (Alain Danielou, 1994). The book discusses, encourages, and tolerates almost every conceivable sexual technique like fellatios, cunnilingus, prostitution, masturbation, anal sex, and even bestiality. It also discusses group sex and homosexuality.

In the Islam world, particularly Pakistan, Afghanistan, and Iran, girls as young as a nine-year-old child are sought by men for a bride because of their tight vaginas. The men would pay the parents of the girl for consenting to the marriage. In his household, the child bride serves the man like a sex slave aside from doing the regular chores. This practice is legal in the Muslim culture but is considered statutory rape in the Western world. Because of poverty and lack of education, prostitution of unmarried young girls is also reported in the Muslim world. The girls don't need a place of business. They are being picked up from the street, and men just take a secluded corner of some business establishments to do the sex act, after which the girls are released with some coins in their hands as payments for their sex service. A group of conservative Muslims asserted that this practice is illegal, but government officials and some religious leaders just did nothing to impose penalties or punishment to those who engaged in this kind of child prostitution. It was said that politicians and some community and religious leaders are among the regular clients of the girls. (NBC News Shahid Qazi and Carol Grisanti, March 24, 2009). Muslim culture and religion requires men and women to observe and honor "hijaab" (dress code). The reason for this dress-code requirement is to minimize sexual enticement and degradation in society as much as possible for both men and women. Virginity is considered an asset of a Muslim woman and every Muslim man expects to marry a woman that is still a virgin. Sex in Islam is a privilege of a man only; and women are treated only as objects of pleasure. (*Abul Kasem*, 8/08/2009). If a woman is raped, such incident would be viewed as caused by her; therefore, she is the one that is being punished because no man would ever do such act if he was not enticed or provoked.

During the time when Mohammed was waging wars with other countries for his newfound faith, he convinced those young men to fight for his cause with a promise that if they died for Allah's sake, Allah will provide them in heaven an abundance of endless pleasure on whatever they sacrificed here on earth (Surah 9:20-22); and that includes sexual pleasure that young men choose to give up for him. Those who survived and were able to go back to their family would also be rewarded with the right to have sex with the widows, including their brothers' widows. Some critics posited that the real reason why Mohammed allowed polygamy was to bring forth more children so that he would not run short of future followers of his newfound religion. Even at present time the practice of having multiple wives is still legal for the same reason, so they would inundate and dominate the world. The issue of having sex with seventy-two virgins in heaven as a reward to those young men who died for Allah has been refuted as not being found anywhere in the Holy Qur'an. Sexual texts and literature are written in other sacred books such as the Tafseer, ahadith Sha'ria, figh, and others.

In Taoism, cunnilingus is a revered sexual practice, much preferred over sexual penetration, because this practice aims to give men and women longevity and vitality. Loss of semen, vaginal and other bodily fluid, is believed to weaken the body. During the Han Dynasty, some Taoist sects considered sexual intercourse as a spiritual practice called *HeQi*, meaning "joining energy." By performing this sexual art, a person could stay in good health, longer life, or attain immortality. In Taoism men are taught how to conserve their life essence through limiting or totally avoiding ejaculation during sexual intercourse. The fluid that contains the most *Jing*, which is the energy-producing substance that prolongs life is the semen and, therefore, must be conserved. Many Taoist practitioners believed that premature aging, disease, and general fatigue are caused by excessive loss of ejaculatory fluids—the life force vital to maintain health. While *HeQi* is Chinese, Tantrism, which is more or less similar in practice with *HeQi*, is a Buddhist and Hindu form of sexual discipline with the same objective, which is to attain immortality by conserving bodily fluids.

In Australia, aboriginal men pay the parents of the baby girl a dowry in exchange for sex when she grows up. Incest is a common tribal practice. The government imposes penalties and punishments on tribal practices and rituals that are banned and considered to be illegal, yet the aborigines in remote places are found still keeping and practicing their usual rituals and beliefs (http://www2.hu-berlin.de/sexolgy/IES/australia.html). In Papua New Guinea, men dominate in their societies; and women are valued as objects to be owned, along with other things like animals, furniture, and others. Domestic violence, rape, prostitution, incest, and teenage sex are ordinary among tribal families. In some areas, plural copulation or group sex is a traditional pattern where a single woman can have sexual intercourse with series of men in tandem. Another notable practice among young males in some tribes is drinking of the male semen as essential for a boy to become a man. It was believed that boys have no semen at all at birth, and it is only through oral insemination from older men can they acquire the necessary semen to become men and to make his offspring survive. Coercive sex or rape is very common in clubs where a woman is forced to have sexual intercourse with a group of men/boys while others watch the event. The girl involved never tells about it because of shame or fear (CCIES at the Kinsey Institute: Papua New Guinea).

When I was young, I saw a movie based on the rituals and beliefs among the natives of Hawaii when a volcano erupts. To appease the gods living there, the natives would make a sacrificial offering to an erupting volcano—the prettiest female virgin in the village, The tribe's spiritual adviser to the king had to accompany the woman to the mouth of the volcano. He would utter some prayers of offering before letting the woman jump. Why sacrifice a woman and not a man? During the primitive days, tribal practices and rituals were sexual in nature; the gods were believed to be males and could only be appeased by a beautiful woman. Sex and marriage rituals involved every member of the tribe with one sole purpose, which was to preserve and protect each other. Intertribal marriages depended on the decision of the tribal chiefs. An outsider had to undergo initiation rites usually conducted by the males of the tribe where the female belongs. Once marriage was approved by all members of the tribe, an alliance was established between the tribes to protect each other from attacks by other tribes. Different practices and beliefs among the Mayas, the Aztecs, the Incas, and the Native American Indians included, among others, a sacrificial offering—either a female animal or a virgin.

During the early days of mankind, it was the female that hunt for their sex partner. When the female was in "heat," she would hunt for a male and forced him to have sex with her. She would choose a man with strong physical features in order to have strong children. The concept of having a family was not in practice because the woman raised the child without a father. Up to the present times, there are groups or communities still dominated by women. It is a practice of the women known as Remo (men) of the Bonda Tribe of Southern India to get a husband about ten to fifteen years younger. When a baby boy is born, his mother receives a dowry in form of money from a woman who wants a husband. The woman raises the boy until manhood and then takes him as her husband. It is their belief that when she becomes old, her young husband will take care of her as a return for taking care of him when he was still a boy. The tribe population decreases in time because the couples could not have children by the time the boy becomes a man and ready for sex; the wife's child-bearing capability is lost because of old age (The Bondas: http://malkangiri.nic.in/Tribes.htm).

Scientology has a different view of human sexuality. According to their founder, L. Ron Hubbard, sex is unnatural for humans and a perversion. It is a tool invented to degrade, created by psychiatrists to trap humans. "Pain and sex" are the stock-in-trade of psychs. Scientology opposes all forms of psychiatry. It says psychiatrists are the sole cause of decline in this universe (http://www.scientology-lies.com/faq/teachings/sex.html). Women members of this group are instructed to stay quite during sexual intercourse, meaning not to make noise in her excitement and also during delivery of her child—that is, not to scream her pain.

Another science-fiction group called Heaven's Gate waited for a sign that would tell them when to commit suicide in order to be liberated from their earthly bodies. They believed they were transient in this earth and soon will be lifted to a "higher place" when the sign arrived which was the Hale-Bopp comet. To overcome one's humanness, which included one's sexuality, they had themselves castrated. The leader Marshall Herff Applewhite, a homosexual, had himself underwent a surgical castration, had a sexual relationship with a man named Bonnie Lu Trusdale Nettles. They called each other nicknames—Tiddy and Wink, Guinea and Piggy, Nincom and Poop, and finally Do and Ti.

In many places all over the world, many more cultures, practices, and rituals involving sex are still being observed. Some groups stick to their usual rituals defying government bans and prohibitions. Others mix old practices with modern ones with some form of modifications and improvements. There are also groups that totally abandoned old practices and adopted new forms of rituals While the civilized world are doing its best to educate and inform tribal minorities to modern and sound sexual practices and rituals, there are some civilized groups in modern times that are still practicing ancient pagan sex rites. (http://www.nowpublic.com/culture/ancient-pagan-sex-rites-praticed-modern-times).

Sex Myths and Superstitions

Sex is no exception to stories of fiction, myths, rumors, and superstitions. Aside from being a favorite topic for jokes, sex still maintains its rank as the most desired activity everyone loves to experience. Some of the vast variety of experiences people encountered in sex becomes legends, myths, and superstition, as they are handed down from generations to generations. These stories are passed on through time already altered, deduced, modified, or expanded. To trace and to prove their authenticity becomes questionable and unreliable because most of them come from tribal practices, agonistic rituals, folklores, and even from jokes.

Pregnancy is one aspect of sex where superstition abounds. To determine the sex of the child inside the womb, the mother has to feel where the baby is mostly settled. If it is high above the belly, it is a girl; and low, a boy. From other sources I heard the reverse—high above the belly, a boy; and below, a girl. If the heartbeat is faster, it is a girl; and slower, a boy. Another way to tell the sex of the child is to hang a wedding ring in a string and put it above the inclined stomach of the pregnant woman. A forward and backward swing of the ring indicates a boy; a circular motion, a girl. A pointed belly means a baby boy; a round belly, a baby girl. A woman doesn't get pregnant when she has sexual intercourse while menstruating. It is also believed that having sex with a woman having menstruation makes a man sick, bald, or even insane. Medical science likewise disproves these beliefs. Husbands are discouraged to have sex with their pregnant wives because it is said that the baby will acquire skin diseases caused by the semen that the husband deposited inside the wife's womb. I witness a relative delivering her baby covered all over with white flaky sediments. The midwife explains that those are the semen of the husband sticking on the baby's skin. Perhaps the reason why husbands are discouraged to have sex with their pregnant wives is for hygienic consideration. Pregnant women are often advised not to look at the eyes of a dog or cat at nighttime; their eyes glow at night that when the child grows up, he/she could see evil spirits at night. Another advice for pregnant women is that, she should not sleep with open windows so that evil spirit could not steal her child while she sleeps. Visiting a funeral when pregnant is prohibited, or the soul of the dead person would reincarnate in the baby she carries. Pregnant women should not bathe in the sea for it is believed that her womb is open, and the sea water gets inside, infecting or drowning her baby. For a pregnant woman to have painless, quick delivery of her baby, rub her belly with snake oil. When my mother delivered their youngest daughter, my father passes on a thread through the needle. If the thread went through at once, the baby will be delivered quickly. Morning sickness and vomiting during pregnancy determine the temper of the baby—a green vomited substance means the baby is bound for greatness; a pink color, excel in arts; black, black sheep of the family; and white, a model child.

Body features and characteristics, as well as hair colors, are said to have sexual significance for the individual. Blondes and redheads are more sexually curious than brunettes. Hairy men are said to have more sexual drive than men without hair. Men with mustache are good kisser and licker. Men with curly hair are violent and temperamental and very aggressive in sex. Men with straight hair are cool lovers. Since our sex organs are private, determining their sizes are often spoken as a joke for speculation. They say that a woman's mouth tells the opening of her vagina—big mouth women has big vaginal opening; small mouth, small opening. Big hips and big butts women are good candidates for motherhood. Women with pouting mouths are said to have fertile sex organs. A female who masturbates very often would have a flat breast. In order for a woman to have bigger boobs, she has to rub over them saps of green papaya; and for nursing mother, a hot papaya soup makes her produce more milk for the baby. When the lips itch, it means someone wants to be kissed. On the male side, the voice is used as a predicator. A man with a loud voice has large testicles and big penis, while a man with small voice has small testicles and small penis. Men with large hands and feet are said to have long and large penis. Longer index finger indicates more supply of estrogen, and the person tends to be neurotic and sensitive, and longer ring finger tells more supply of testosterone and could reveal hyperactive and aggressive personality. If an index finger is longer than the ring finger, the person is gay.

I have a male cousin who is said to have only one testicle. Children of his age, including his siblings, would make fun of him. It is believed that boys/men with one testicle could not have a child, meaning he would become sterile and could not father a baby. Medical science disproves this belief. Testicles are not responsible for reproduction; semen that carries the sperm is. It is the sperm count and its temperature that determine reproductive capability of a man. Testicles only serve as storage where semen is produced. Another testicle myth was that if a man has only the right testicles, he would have male children; and if he has the left testicle, he would have baby girls.

Sometimes parents are also good source of sex myths and superstition. To discourage their daughter from dating, they would tell her that kissing can make her pregnant and that she could contract venereal diseases from the toilets or the seats in a dark movie house. Girls are told not to swim in a swimming pool with the boys, or they could get pregnant because boys released their semen in the water, which could travel into the girl's vagina. To check if a girl is a virgin, boys are told to take with him a white tissue paper when having sex with her and use it to wipe the vagina. She is a virgin if she bled. Young boys are also told that masturbation could cause acne, blindness, epilepsy, insanity, nosebleeds, or warts and, if done abusively by men, may cause impotency because of excessive pressure on the nerves of the penis. Boys should not urinate outside at night. Evil spirits will cut his penis because they are attracted to small penis. Girls should not urinate outside at night because evil spirits will impregnate her.

Flirting and lovemaking also have a long list of myths and superstitions. To arouse a man, the woman has to tickle the area between the anus and the scrotum of a man and the tip of his penis, but to tickle the nose or the ears with an index finger doubles the arousal of a man. To suggest to a woman to have sex with her, the man tickles with his point finger the center of her palm while shaking hands. If she does not pull her hand and she looks at the man, it means she accepts the suggestion. Another way to invite a woman for sex is to rub his hand on her knee calf; if she looks at the man, she accepts the suggestion. If you immediately stand up after sex, you can not get pregnant. To have a baby girl, the husband should not push too much in the lovemaking; if he wants a boy, he should have a very deep penetration. Women who swallow semen in oral sex will have throat cancer. Oral sex and anal sex are the causes of AIDS because the germs mix with the semen become destructive, attacking the immune system.

Love potions, amulets, and aphrodisiacs are classified as superstition because most of them don't have scientific explanations. To make a man go crazy in love with a woman, she should rinse her used panty and use the water to mix with a soda then let him drink it. Braiding a loose pubic hair of a man and carrying it in the purse attract more men. It is said that when a woman is in "heat," she emits a particular smell coming from the vagina that attracts the male species. Other females cannot recognize the smell, only the opposite sex. Perfume makers called this scent pheromone. During my high school days, my classmates and I have this belief that to make our crushes fall in love with us, we have to get a hair of the boy and clip it in between our pictures to make the boy think of us every minute. To make a suitor propose marriage to their daughter, parents take a single hair of their daughter and submerge it in the lemonade or soda then serve it to the guy. If the suitor is invited to dine with the family, a hair of the girl in his soup will make him propose marriage within a week. Most popular aphrodisiacs being sought by men is the oysters and some ethnic seafood, like the sea urchin and clams.

Widows and widowers are also the target of sex jokes and superstitions. It is said that a woman who married several times have teeth in her vagina. This is the reason why she lost several husbands; she excites him so much when having intercourse with her that makes him sick instead. Medical science has never discovered the presence of teeth in those types of women. It could be that the origin of this story was idiomatic in nature. The term "vaginas with teeth" is said to mean capable of cutting someone's life due to excessive sexual excitement. Widower version is that the man has blades on his penis that when he had intercourse with his wife, the wife bleeds to death. None of these stories were found to be true.

Wedding events are also sources of superstitions and myths. Stepping on one's partner's shoe while dancing will tell who dominates in the marriage. Catching the bouquets of the bride means the catcher is the next bride, and the guy who catches the bride's garter belt means he is the next groom. When I asked my father what was his belief when he let me drink the water with an egg soaked overnight, he said it was for fertility.

One early morning when I woke up, I saw a group of townspeople rushing toward the hospital located next to our neighbor on the right side. The news was that a couple was admitted to the hospital in an emergency situation because for hours, after their sexual intercourse, the man cannot pull out his penis from the woman's sex organ. It was rumored that the wife of the man sprayed semen of a stingray to the brief of her husband. She was suspicious that her husband was having an affair with the woman now admitted with her husband in the hospital. It was a belief I always hear from adults that the semen of a male stingray has a gluey characteristics, thus, has the possibility to stick onto a surface in contact. The irony about the commotion over the news was that when those curious people came out from the hospital, they only said that the couples were already separated and needed privacy. So no one really saw the couple in a "connected status." Even until now people still think such incidence really happened.

Every culture—Hindu, Chinese, Persian, Greek, Romans, Arabians, and all others—have their own version of the story of creation. What is common in all these stories of creation is that there are two sexes being created, the male and the female. To the unbelievers, the story of Adam and Eve is only a myth. Rumors, superstitions, myths, and jokes about sex invite curiosity, making anyone ask the question: are all of these true? Some of them could be factual, but nobody cares to trace their authenticities and their scientific support. As these myths, beliefs, and superstition are passed on through time from generations to generations, most of them would surely undergo some minor or major deviations from the original—probably to fit the mind-set of their time.

Insanity and Sex

After school, after three o'clock in the afternoon, most kids went straight to their houses to help their parents. Only few stayed in the school compound to play. One afternoon, I stayed to play baseball with my classmates. At one time when the ball went outbound as far as the fishpond outside the perimeter of the school, the runner noticed something moving behind the banana trees. He called us to take a look at what he discovered. We all rushed to find a fully naked man hiding among the banana trees, playing with his genitals and enjoying it. His genitals looked swollen and red. Some kids threw stones at him, while the others screamed to scare him. When he noticed us, he hurriedly gathered his clothes, covered his genitals, and then sped away. He was scared and crying loud like a baby deprived of his favorite toy. We knew the man as the crazy homeless guy who always chased little children in the neighborhood, or sometimes being chased by little children as they made fun of him. I was not bothered about his crying and speeding away. What intrigue me was why did he enjoy playing with his genitals? From what I saw, it seemed like his genitals were inflamed caused by constant rubbing. I heard from my playmates that he was always seen doing that in any place he could hide in. What kind of pleasure was he getting from this? Did he do it because he was attracted to a woman? Or he just found pleasure in rubbing his genitals, as if it were a plaything?

Another incident similar to this happened during my teens. One evening about midnight, a loud scream of a woman was heard coming from the town's tennis court. Having no electricity yet at that time, no one could figure out what was happening inside the tennis court. My father who worked as a policeman went to the place to find out the source of the scream. He saw teenage kids taking turns raping the woman. He stopped and tried to apprehend them, but they were scattered faster than my father could hold. He took the woman to the municipal building and instructed the night guard to give the woman a place to sleep for the night. Early morning I saw the woman sitting on the bench outside my parents' dress shop. I presumed she came to thank my father for saving her last night. She was happy humming her song while she busied herself sewing empty cement bags for her clothing. My mother supplied her with needle and thread but not the scissors; she cut the thread with her teeth. In between her humming a song, she was talking to herself, sometimes laughing, sometimes crying, or sometimes getting angry at an invisible enemy. I sat beside her to ask questions what happened last night. "I heard you screaming last night. What happened?" I asked politely. "The boys did something to me," she replied. "Did you like it?" I asked in a friendly tone. She gave a big nod, indicating a positive answer. "Then why did you scream?" I followed up. She stopped sewing her paper cloth then stared at me with raging look. "I told you I liked it . . . I liked it . . . I liked it . . ." stretching the last sentence with an irritating voice. She threw away what she was doing and ran away crying. Confused and baffled, I asked myself, "Why did she cry if she liked it?" The townspeople learned that the woman had a miscarriage but could not accept that she lost her baby. She roamed from one town to another searching for her baby and oftentimes missed eating food, thus, aggravating her mental state. Oftentimes she would be seen chasing teenage boys at daytime, and in the nighttime young boys practice sex with her, which she probably like but with a scream. The next day after the interview, I saw her exposing her bare breast to a group of young boys that she was chasing about. My parents believed that if she were given regular meals, she could probably have a chance of recovering her sanity. After my parents regularly fed her, she recovered and later worked as a cook for a beauty-saloon owner in the city.

During my short visit in my province in 2008, I went to view the new renovated Cebu Cathedral. On my way inside, I passed by a fully naked woman sitting by the gate of the cathedral. I saw a woman hand her a piece of clothing to cover her body, but the crazy woman refused. She preferred to be seen naked. My question is why she chose, of all places, a sacred place such as the cathedral and why did she refuse the clothes that was given to her. One of the answers I gathered from sources was that she wanted to scandalize the religious people who she believed condemned and cursed her because she was a prostitute. It was also said that at night, she would let any man had sex with her at the church ground.

My mother also had a story about her laundrywoman who one day ran to her for help because her husband threatened to burn their house. The laundrywoman said that she was ironing the clothes overnight when her husband demanded sex from her. Tired and overworked, she just ignored him. Early in the morning, the husband ranted outside, holding a can of petroleum, ready to pour them around the house to burn it. She gathered whatever she could carry and run for help. The neighbors intervened and prevented the husband from burning his house. Later that night he apologized and enamored his wife with sex. Why did the husband behave in such manner, disregarding the importance of their house over a repressed sex desire? Could such behavior be classified as insanity? There was also one incident I recalled when a neighbor was heard screaming because her husband threw empty wine bottles on their windows. According to her statement when the police arrived, her husband was always like that whenever she refuses sex with him and would sometimes run naked around the neighborhood shouting obscene words.

In one occasion during a birthday party, one friend told us how her husband would throw tantrums whenever he wanted sex with her. Shy to ask for sex with her, her husband would tire himself by fetching water, filling up all jugs he could find in the house, then he would empty the jugs one by one, and fill up again until he got tired. If she made a comment to stop him, he threw things and screamed at her. That was his way of telling her that he wanted sex. In another incident during my high school days, a man was seen bleeding beside a dumpster. When approached by the police, he was already losing blood, almost unconscious, and was rushed to the hospital. When interviewed about what he did, he said he just cut his penis because it has no use anymore; his wife left him.

Unreciprocated affection to the opposite sex, deprivation of sexual needs, or rejection often drives men to insanity and sometimes to commit crime. In suburban Pittsburg, Pennsylvania, George Sodini, a forty-eight-year-old loner went in rampage by killing women in a fitness gym. Before killing himself, he made a video inviting the women to see his place to consider the possibility of marrying him. It was learned from his video that he never had sex for a long time, and he was looking for a woman to be his wife. Frustrated from not finding one, he went on a killing rampage then killed himself. During my first year in college, I recall an incident where a rejected lover followed the object of his affection in school, caught her on the stairway, stabbed her, and then turned the knife on him. Talks spread that the girl broke up with him as ordered by her parents because the guy came from a poor family. A year after, a rejected pregnant woman, after giving a farewell note to her lover, jumped from the fourth floor of the university where the guy was studying. It was humored that the guy would not marry her and did not accept the baby to be his. What is in repressed sexual desires that drive a person crazy? Why do people behave in such manner, as if sex is the only reason for their living?

There was a fellow male teacher who I thought was really preoccupied with sex. Every time he was around with female teachers, he would always make sexual remarks such as: "Your legs make me have an erection," or "Hmmm . . . you smell so good, my down under could smell you." As he said that, he touched his crotch and released a loud laughter. Today such remarks are classified as sexual harassment, but not during our time. We just ignored those instances and stayed away from him. For us he was just a sexually obsessed crazy guy.

There was an unmarried man in our neighborhood that was always seen exposing and rubbing his penis to any woman he finds in a packed crowd. All that the women could do was to move away from him whenever he was seen around. My younger sisters also had the same experience inside a packed movie house. The man behind her stuck out his penis and rubbed it to her back. When she got home, she found at the back of her blouse some white, sticky, almost dried liquid, probably the semen of the man who was behind her in the packed movie house. Indecent exposure or exhibitionism in public could also be considered insanity because the person doing such act is presumed to be not in his sound judgment. Many men, including some celebrities, have been caught exposing to children at the park, in school parking lots, and in any other places. Streaking has also been reported in places where large number of people, like stadium and arenas, are gathered. Other forms of perversions such as sadism, masochism, bestiality, necrophilia, and others are manifestations of an insane mind.

State facilities for persons with mental retardation encounter several problems relating to the sexual activities of the residents. Problems such as tolerating sexual contacts between the male and female residents in the facility, giving contraceptives, aborting unwanted pregnancy, or sterilizing the patient are the most common problem listed. It has been observed in those institutions that residents there have sexual urges on a regular basis and in their heightened stage. Every State has their own rules and regulations in handling mentally deficient citizens. The issue on the patient's ability to give consent—because they are mentally impaired versus the issue on their rights to privacy and because they are human beings with rights—has been the subject of endless debate among caregivers and government officials; to work toward a uniform and standard rules and policies for all state hospitals is the focus of the debate. The question about the rights and privileges of these mentally ill residents could probably have a compromised solution, but how do we deal with physical needs and their consequences. What caused these mentally deficient citizens to have the urge to copulate? Which part of the brain is responsible for such a compelling urge? What really goes on inside their brain that made them behave like someone insane and disoriented, yet seem like normal in their sexual needs and desires? A close friend who has studied psychiatry had this as an explanation why insane individuals still engage in sexual intercourse. She said an insane person has lucid moments sometimes. At this moment they think normal just like anyone. In their lucid moment, they feel isolated, unwanted, and neglected because society treats them as crazy. In their awareness of being isolated, they long, wish, or crave for intimacy; and to them sex is the answer to this desire to be with somebody.

It would be very intriguing to note why mentally impaired individual still has the urge to have sex. Not only in monitored places are unwanted pregnancies happening, but also in places where the insane is left wandering on the streets. Many wandering women get pregnant by men who took advantage of their insanity. There was an instance when we saw an insane woman running with blood dripping through her legs. It was said she just have delivered a baby in the dumpster. Mostly this poor woman encountered someone or some group who would rape her in secluded places. What drives a sane person to have sex (rape) with a woman with mental problems? What part of his brain is responsible for such behavior?

In the movie *One Flew Over the Cuckoo's Nests*, the character played by Jack Nicholson, Randle Patrick McMurphy, a gambler and a con man, faked insanity in order to be admitted to a mental ward. He made a stir in the mental institution with his rebellious personality, one of which was to make Billy Bibit, a stutterer, experience sex for the first time with his prostitute friend, Candy. Billy was able to talk straight after the experience for a short while but was back to his usual stuttering when the nurse threatened to tell his mother. Billy eventually committed suicide. Is sexual experience a remedy to make a mentally disturbed person confident of himself? Should sex be permitted in a mental ward if such is the case? Seeing Billy talking straight for the first time after having sex and going back to stuttering when threatened, should we say that sexual deprivation caused a person to become insane and only a sexual intercourse can make an insane person feels normal again? Is this why they do it again and again just to be normal?

Sex and the Brain

In my years of curious journey into the world of sex, I found it perturbing to reconcile the devil, sin, sex, and the brain. I often heard my parents say that an idle mind is the workshop of the devil, meaning the devil has access to the brain (mind) and influences it to commit a sin, including the sin of sexual desires. Is the brain responsible for the sexual activity of a person, or the devil?

The brain is the center of the human nervous system. Its structure and its functions are so complicated. It functions like the CPU (central processing unit) of a computer, except that the brain has added features, such as having logic and the ability to express emotions. Unlike the CPU in the computer, the brain is a conscious machine, aware of what is happening in and outside of its perimeter. The five senses, including intuition, sometimes called the sixth sense, act as the keyboard that inputs information to the brain. The information passes through the spinal cords then to the respective sections of the brain. It stores the past experiences we have had, the present activities, and even speculates future events in forms of wishful thinking, fantasies, and daydreaming. At the point of fetus formation inside the mother's womb, the brain when developed is just like a blank tape. Medical science found out through research that as early as three weeks old inside the womb of the mother, right after the brain is fully developed, the brain picks up every detail activity inside and outside of the fetus's body. It can hear sounds, and it can feel the emotional state of its host, which is the mother. Pregnant mothers are even encouraged to play classical music within touching distance with her belly, sing a song while patting the belly, and not to fight so the baby could not pick up fear. After birth, the child's brain records in detail the different stimuli around him/her, including those that are sexual, like when given a bath or a diaper change—the caregiver's hands have contact with the sexual organs. The baby's brain identifies this particular part, the sexual organ, to be the most sensitive of all. The brain records this as pleasurable. A child's judgment, which is either to accept or reject eroticism from any source, determines his sexuality. Example, the child identifies only the mother as the source of eroticism and decided to let it stay that way, then this child will have a very strong maternal fixation; this was posited as a factor for homosexuality. If the child accepts other sources of eroticism, he would have multiple fixations—to the father, mother, or a relative or friend—and surely would be heterosexual when he/she grows up. The levels of eroticism are decoded in accordance to the degree of pleasurable stimulation experienced from each person.

On the other hand, the human mind receives a different treatment when it comes to understanding and analyzing behavior. While behavior is the outward manifestation of what is going on inside the human brain, we cannot disregard the fact that what is in the mind, as well, is responsible for such a behavior. Whatever is recorded and stored in our human brain distinguishes us from the other. What is the mind then? How does the mind develop? Dr. Daniel J. Siegel, author of the book *The Developing Mind: How Relationships and the Brain Interact to Shape Who We Are*, gives us a scholarly overview, exploring a wide range of scientific discipline, on how the human mind emerges at the interface of interpersonal experience and the structure and function of the brain. All the experiences recorded shape the brain and, thus, organize the mind. The brains of the serial killers stored memories of rejections, hate, anger, revenge, and violence. When these are transformed into action, we can begin counting dead bodies of victims. A child sexually traumatized and could not rationalize the circumstances of his traumas has in her memories anger, confusion, fear, and hate. When this child becomes an adult, his actions will tell a painful past, becomes antisocial, and probably will kill or become a pedophile. Children who were fondled sexually and loved it would possibly become promiscuous adult seeking sexual pleasure obsessively. The prostitutes and the pornographers who never experienced a loving relationship with the opposite sex store memories of regrets and low self-esteem. When we meet them on the streets, we could either see a downtrodden person; who avoids eye contact, or an overly defensive flirt. A young soldier who has never killed a rat and was assigned to Iraq or to Afghanistan to kill the enemy could manifest guilt and confusion and could possibly end up killing himself or killing others. When I was five years old, an old guy attempted to molest me, but it did not register a trauma in my mind because it was aborted by my father who was looking for me. The early exposure I have at age seven when I saw two adults having sex, when my ex-boyfriend attempted to rape me at age sixteen, and the pornographic materials I read and typed at age seventeen, shaped and formed my attitude and understanding of sex. I became wary and fearful of the opposite sex that I did not date until I was twenty-three years old and have finished college.

Many scientists, particularly in the medical field, conducted numerous researches on the relationship between the brain and sexual activities of humans. The results and findings in these researches were oftentimes in agreement; however, we could not ignore the fact that there were researches of the same subject that were somehow contrasting in discipline and opinion. With regard to human sexuality, everybody agreed that the brain plays in all aspect a major role in the sexual activity of humans, being their most important sexual organ. The limbic system or paleomammalian brain, often referred to as the emotional brain, is a set of brain structures, including the hippocampus, amygdala, anterior thalamic nuclei, and limbic cortex, which support a variety of functions, including autobiographical consciousness, activation of arousal or emotion, social information or behavior, long-term memory or coordination of bodily response and higher cognitive processing, and olfaction, the process of smelling. Amygdala, an almond-shaped area near the hypothalamus, plays a role in sexual arousal in human beings and also in the lower animal species. Medical scientists are exploring the possibilities that genetics also plays a major role in the sexual behavior of an individual. The question to abort children of murderers, prostitutes, and insane individuals for fear of them becoming such is still very much debated.

Two and a half years ago, LeVay, then a neurobiologist at the Salk Institute in La Jolla, California, made a sensational finding in the differences between homosexuals and heterosexual men in their brain area. In his experimental research conducted on forty-one people—nineteen homosexual men, sixteen heterosexual men, and six women—he found that the largest INAH3 cluster belongs to heterosexual men, the smallest to gay men, which were of the same size range as that of women's. The same is true with the amygdala; it is larger in the male specie than in the female specie. Dr. LeVay encounters many opposing opinions from other professionals with regard to his findings, but the public response was encouraging (http://discovermagazine.com/1994/mar/sexandthebrain346).

Neurochemistry identified the different chemicals found in the brain that trigger or lower sexual urges. Are the supplies or flow of the different hormones—testosterone and estrogen and other neurochemicals, such as dopamine, prolactin, serotonin, endorphin, and oxytocin—cause the person to have or not have sexual urges? Or is it the outside stimuli, like seeing a naked body or an adult movie or smelling a turnoff odor that sends signals to the brain that would then signal to release the appropriate chemicals to activate the responses? Why does the male body respond by releasing semen while dreaming of sexual intercourse? What chemicals are being released while the person was sleeping and having wet dream. Several medical studies have been conducted about brain activities and the related chemicals released during sexual attraction, sexual intercourse, and orgasm. While the regions of the brain had been located similarly on every case study as well as the kind of chemicals being released, the behavior of the patients differs (Your Brain and Sex, http://www.reuniting.info/science/sex_in_the_brain).

In the movie *Away from Her* (2006), the female character played by Julie Christie experiences a total loss of her memories (Alzheimer) yet remains vibrant in her sexual life. While this could be explained by medical science—that is, memory and sexual needs have different compartments in the brain—one would ask, whether or not her husband's cheating past was a deliberate cause of her memory loss and the sexual attraction to another man as a vindication? Was it the emotion that was painfully affected, being hurt and wishing for vindication that made some part of the brain link with the memory and the desire to be loved? It is a proven fact, whether having memory loss or not, that individuals with mental disorientation still desire to connect physically with the opposite sex.

Sexual perversion such as sadism, masochism, necrophilia, bestiality, and other abnormal sexual expressions, regardless how mild, are manifestations of a brain's capability to function beyond reason and logic—a manifestation of a disoriented personality, a result of a dysfunctional relationship. Psychiatry explained this as caused by some chemical imbalance in the brain. The book *The Developing Mind: How Relationships and the Brain Interact to Shape Who We Are* by Daniel J. Siegel, MD, meticulously studied and examined various factors that comprise the total personality of a person from time of conception to old age, combining neurobiology, research psychology, and cognitive science; how the brain/mind chronicles all kinds of relationship as it develops and shapes the total person.

While medical science explains the working of the brain/mind as caused by the circumstances experienced by man; the religious groups attributed to the devil the evils that man does particularly those related to sexual urges and desires. The explanation to this begins with the devil who knows that sexual intercourse between a man and a woman is a creative gift from God, and he was never given such gift. This could be the reason why he rebelled against God and was cast to hell. The devil was jealous of man and angry at God. After the devil triumphed in tempting Adam and Eve to have sex the lustful way and ignore God's plan, man has to confront a struggle or a war inside his very nature as a person. His soul wants to express love with tenderness, protection, compassion, and the desire to protect and to suffer for the beloved; but his beastly nature wants to tear up, to grab, to bite, to suck, to scratch, to express lust. That is why we see men who are kind, compassionate, and tender in their relationship with a woman when having sex and we also see some men who are so brutal, inconsiderate, and violent in expressing their sexual connection with a woman. These two opposing behaviors of man are inherent in his nature but what he choose to prevail in his action tells how his mental state was shaped in his brain.

Human Dignity and Sex

When the life of a fetus inside a mother's womb is cut short through abortion, human dignity becomes a question on the mother who consents to it, on the abortionist who performs it, and on the community who condones it. Depriving a helpless human being the right to life is abominable, no matter what justification one could come up with. There could be a long list of personal reasons why a mother chooses abortion, but the innermost reason is the fear of raising another human being in this kind of economic uncertainties and insecurities that the world is in. The fear just overwhelms the person who is responsible to raise this child. The reality of the world population exploding to a shocking number just scares these helpless mothers. These women who choose abortion are acting, as if they have done the world a great favor. It is just like saying "before the bees and the worms and the sun and the storm waste away a flower that could someday be a tall tree, it is better to nip it at the bud."

Other women claim sole ownership of their body that to conceive and to give birth to a child is an invasion to her personal rights and privacy as a person. Contraception and the desire not to raise children in marriage become an unwritten vow in a marriage ceremony nowadays. We fight for benefits, freedom, health, privileges, rights, wealth, and the list goes on in order for us to survive in this world; but survival has to be measured on how we value ourselves and others. This value or self-worth is what we called dignity. We claim dignity in the workplace, in our employment; we claim dignity in our community, demanding respect and privacy of our personal lives; we claim dignity everywhere to make us enjoy the rights and privileges of being a person. Such is so valuable to us that we could even kill anyone who steals it from us or tramples on it; yet, ironic though, it is so easy nowadays to lose it or even offer ourselves to lose it for the pleasure of sex. How many reputable men and women we know who are forced to give up their fame and prestige after being discovered or exposed as living a double life: an admirable priests exposed for child molestation, a smart doctor who raped or fondled his own patients, an excellent educator who seduced his fourteen-year-old student, a politician having an affair with his secretary, a successful evangelical who frequented a prostitution house, an ideal father who spent wee hours at night viewing pornography, and so on.

One aspect of human dignity that has gone awry is the total disregard to the sanctity of the human body. Our faith told us that our body is the temple of the Holy Spirit and that anyone who destroys this temple, he/she would God destroy (1 Cor. 3:16-17). Sexuality in our modern setting is no longer an act of self-giving or as an expression of love, in which we accept each other completely as the fore bearer of a new life brought forth in the union. It becomes depersonalized and exploited, appearing merely as an occasion for self-gratification and for pleasure. The body appears to be a tool to be utilized for one's well-being, the main purpose of which is to figure out how to draw the greatest profit or the highest pleasure from it. Society's market is flooded with calendars of nude men and women, movies depicting sexual torture and perversion, Internet overloaded with pornographic sites, television with bedroom scenarios showing couples, married or unmarried, doing sex, and musical world depicting perverted dance moves intended to sexually arouse the viewers.

What can we say to a nine-year-old girl becoming a bride of an older person with one sole purpose, which is to have sexual gratification because of her tight vagina? This kind of marriage is said to be legal in some Muslim countries such as Pakistan, Afghanistan, Iraq, and Iran. Not only are these girls being treated as sex slaves, they are also made to work like slaves in the house. We heard from televisions and radios and read from daily newspapers about domestic abuses by husbands on his wife and children. Many would agree that even in married couples, human dignity is being downgraded or trampled upon by husbands in many different ways through domestic violence and sexual slavery. Sometimes peace officers are caught in-between. Should not the husbands be concerned of the well-being of his family? Why destroy the very "household" that he is supposed to protect? I met one time a young woman who confided to me how her husband would demand oral sex from her and, when aroused, would spread all over her face his semen as he swings his penis. I saw this scenario in the many pornographic sites I visited in the Internet. Is this what the husband vowed to cherish and protect during their wedding ceremony? What kind of a husband is he who promised to love and cherish his wife and then treats her this way? What about old age, what kind of memoirs this couple would recollect when their "sunset" comes? She said she was so belittled and so ashamed to work because she acquired herpes, a result of purposely not cleaning his genitals and the surrounding area. She said his game was to let her clean the surrounding part of his crotch by licking before she does the oral sex. Sodomy was also performed on her. At present time, they are undergoing a divorce proceeding.

Another wife, a friend, confided to me that whenever they had a fight with her husband, which included physical abuse, while she was still in tears, her husband would use sex to calm her down. She would just submit to the act like a log because if she refused him, she would get another beating or he would have tantrums. He never asked any apology every time he did this to her. It could probably be his way of saying he was sorry for what he did. In another instance way back in the '70s, there was a prominent but notorious businessman in our town who always brought prostitutes to the beach and left them without clothes until morning. Added to that, it was said that this man would insert into the woman's vagina a spool of thread, then slowly pulling the thread out as she wiggled and waggled helplessly and in pain. Sometimes he would throw inside her vagina a handful of beach sands. The young peeping Toms in our community who enjoyed watching what this man and his bodyguards did to the prostitutes were the source of this talk.

It is despicable to see in the pornographic sites in the Internet a woman kneeling in front of a man standing while she does oral sex on him. It is like seeing a dog being made to bite a bone that has no meat. We can tell by looking at the facial expressions of some women in the pornography business that they performed such act against their will. Forcing or paying somebody to have sex against their will is stripping one's dignity as a person. In another view I saw a young prostitute being picked up by three young men for sex; all three did oral, vaginal, and anal sex with her simultaneously. After the act, the three men paid her fake dollar bills; they run away laughing as the prostitute chased them.

Humans are capable of creating limitless forms and ways of attaining sexual pleasure, often disregarding consequences that include spiritual well-being of an individual and sexually transmitted diseases. Wife-swapping, sex-trafficking, all forms of perversions, free sex, masturbation, pornography, prostitution, all these are forms of debasement—physically, emotionally, and spiritually. Ridiculing or bashing gay individuals is also one form of degradation and disrespect of their dignity.

Anthropology provides us a clear understanding of the nature of man and his physical, social, material, and cultural development, including his origins, evolution, geographic distribution, ethnology, and communal forms. For Charles Darwin and his followers, humans are descendants of the apes whose intellectual faculties are mere developed animal power (but apes and monkeys are not brutal in their sexual acts). In the Bible man is a living creature created in the image and likeness of God. He is given the privilege to be the child of God and heir to the kingdom of heaven. He has the faculty of speech and is capable of reasoning. To the theologians, man is a composite of body and soul; the body expresses the material characteristic; and the soul, the spiritual. As to his material part, sacred writings declared that God formed him from dust and breathed into his face the breath of life, making him a living soul (Gen. 2:7). This elevates us from all other forms of creatures God has ever made. When we see the dignity of one another, when we see the person's attributes embedded in his person, we begin to love the person (Pope John Paul II's *Theology of the Body*).

Human nature is dualistic. Man is capable of violence, brutality, hatred, anger, greed, lust, and many more; likewise, he can be calm, compassionate, loving, generous, virtuous, and many more. What makes man dignified is the fact that God created him in his image and likeness, put him above all forms of creation, endowed him with free will, breathed into him a soul that gave him eternal life, and most of all made him an heir to his kingdom. Based on Pope John Paul II's *Theology of the Body*, Christopher West conducted a series of lectures and conferences on the need for all of humanity to value and to respect one another, if we are to find the purpose and meaning of our existence, and to find the final destination in our journey to life. The audiotapes *The Dignity of Man: An Introduction to the Anthropology of John Paul II, John Paul II and Sacramental Sex: What Hollywood Doesn't Know and Your Parents Never Told You*, and *Created and Redeemed: The Universal Message of John Paul II's Theology of the Body* point to us the undeniable truth that we are made in the image and likeness of God. Our experiences should lead us ultimately to God. We have to know who we are interiorly before we can penetrate into the objective reality of who we are.

By definition, dignity is the state or quality of being excellent, worthy, or honorable—having a stately bearing, stateliness, distinction. These definitions are mere words, which do not truly describe what real dignity is unless the human person experiences it. I recall a simple incident that I witness years ago that really enraged my heart when I saw a father stripping his four-year-old son of his dignity. The little boy was chased around by the nanny as she asked the boy to drink water after eating. The boy must have been enjoying the chase as he run around the dining and the living room. The father was annoyed that he took the glass of water from the nanny and grabbed the boy on his arm and forced him to drink. The boy refused and managed to let loose from his grip. When the father caught him again, he forced the glass of water to his mouth. When the boy refused, the father poured all the water on his son's head, making him wet all over. The boy looked around to see if there was anyone who saw him got wet. He was so ashamed that he run to his room and locked himself in. A four-year-old boy knew then he was being stripped of his dignity as a child.

Another incident I gathered came from a wife who unloaded to me what her husband did to her. They were riding on a public transportation when some issues came about that caused them to have a small argument while the other passengers were listening.

The husband got mad that he forced the wife to kneel before all the passengers inside a running vehicle until they reached home. She had to kneel against her will, or she would be kicked out from a running vehicle. She was so humiliated that while kneeling, she just looked down and sobbed silently as tears rolled down her cheeks. The husband never apologized. These and many more situations of humiliations are happening everywhere. We could not rationalize why there are people who enjoy degrading and debasing their fellow coheirs to God's kingdom. What and who gave them that privilege?

For what reason did Jesus Christ die on the cross but to redeem mankind from sin and restore in them the right to God's kingdom. Are we really worth dying for if we don't mean anything to God? God so loved the world that he gave his only beloved son so that everyone who believes in him might not perish but might have eternal life. God did not send his Son into the world to condemn the world but that the world might be saved through him (John 3:16-17). First we have to ask, "Did Jesus Christ really come to the world. Did he really exist?" Historians, not theologians, attested that Jesus Christ was a real person walking around Jerusalem, preaching the good news called Gospels. He did not gather men, did not arm them with swords, and did not cross countries, beheading anyone who did not believe in him; he was preaching love of God and love of neighbors. He did not have enemies but was put to death because he was different. His ministry was centered on man's final destiny, which is the kingdom of God. When he said he would destroy the temple and rebuild it in three days, he did not mean the physical building in Jerusalem people called the Temple. The temple that he meant is the human body; the temple where the Holy Spirit dwells. This truth is what makes man dignified. We are worth dying for because God created us out of love. He loves us because we are his children, and as children we are the heirs to his kingdom in heaven. Before God, all of us are equal and there is no justification for any one to strip us of our inalienable right to live and to pursue happiness.

Part IV

Theology: The Truth beyond Human Nature

For those who live according to the flesh

are concerned with the things of the flesh, but

those who live according to the spirit

are concerned with the things of the spirit.

The concern of the flesh is death, but

the concern of the spirit is life and peace.

—Letter to the Romans 8:5-6

The Creator and Sex

The void is in total darkness, yet it seems something in there exists. This something said, "Let there be light," and there was light, but still he could not be seen. He is in the darkness and also in the brightness. To the scientists and the atheists, he is the energy, the force, the power that moves the universe. To the mortals, he is their creator; to the believers, he is their God. This God is called Yahweh or Elohim by the Jewish people, Allah by the Muslims, Jehovah to a certain religious sect, Eli or Father by Jesus Christ and his followers. He has many other names descriptive of his nature like the Almighty, the Merciful, the Absolute Power, the Prime Mover, the Omniscient, and countless more. There is only one God as we are told in our religion. He is the beginning, and he is the end — the Alpha and the Omega. He could be anywhere and everywhere without someone knowing because he is invisible. But how do we know God? We do not hear his voice. Is he a man, a woman, or both?

Jesus Christ addressed God as "my father," therefore, he is a male. But why are there some philosophers and theologians who postulated that God is asexual; to others, that God is a female; to some others, that God is a male; and still to others, that God is both male and female. In the audiotape version of the book *Conversation with God: an uncommon dialogue* by Neale Donald Walsch (1996), we hear the voice of a female god alternating with the voice of a male god — a telling that God can be a male or a female. But in his book *What God Wants: A Compelling Answer to Humanity's Biggest Question*, Neale Donald Walsch (2005) tells us that God has no gender at all. The terms "male" and "female" are used to address sexuality of a created being. Sex as a gift from God is a tool to reproduce and propagate the species—to multiply, as what God has commanded to all creatures. God does not need to multiply and preserve his specie; therefore, the question whether God is a male or female is irrelevant. God is asexual. When we used the pronoun "he," which is masculine, in referring to God, the reason is purely semantics.

In *God: A Biography*, Jack Miles, the author, attributed to God the characteristics that are apparently masculine in nature—that of being a destroyer, a liberator, a lawgiver, a liege, a conqueror, a father, an architect, an arbiter, an executioner, and more. Jack Miles took the literary route of personifying God, taking in context the Bible as a literary work. His text references and analysis were based on the Hebrew Bible or *Tanakh*, known to us Christians as the Old Testament, the book said to be authored by God. When God created Adam in his image and likeness, he gave to Adam his characteristics, and looking at Adam's physical features and characteristics, he is all male; therefore, God is a male. The attributes of Adam proved that God is a man, If God was a woman, the first human would have been Eve as we would have seen in her attributes. The purpose of Adam's creation in the first place, according to Miles, was that God needs a companion. He gave Adam dominion over all of his creation, even giving him the privilege to name each of them. But God found Adam to be lonely and did not find happiness with the other creations, similar to what he felt being alone. So he put Adam into a deep sleep, and from his ribs he created a being that had the characteristic complimentary to what he and Adam had: compassionate (destroyer), follower (lawgiver), mother (father), subject (conqueror), listener (arbiter), forgiver (executioner), and more. These are the attributes inherent in the other being that he created whom Adam called "woman." The feminine attributes, though weaker compared to the male attributes, are powerful because the male desires the female; and to have her, by his own loving intention, he offers to be subdued by the female—that is, to submit to the wishes of the female. It is his love for the woman that makes man weaker. Man will always seek a woman that is why he leaves his father and mother and joins with her, and the two will become one flesh. When Eve offered the apple to Adam to eat, he did not question her; he just took it and ate it.

From the story of creation, we learned that God created the beast, the insects, and all other creatures together as male and female. Why didn't God create Adam and Eve at the same time? Why was Eve created later, and why did God put Adam into a deep sleep when he created Eve? Why did God take a rib from Adam and made it a woman instead of a scoop of dust? Was Adam already a male when God created him? If he was, then God had already in mind to create a woman. If Adam's sexuality was decided when God found him to be needy of a companion, then that could explain why he was put to a deep sleep. Perhaps God made a major repair on Adam's body. The story of the creation of man narrates only how life on earth began, but it did not even tell why. Bible scholars, theologians, and philosophers gave us only one reason why God created mankind: he was alone, and he wanted to be known. In his creating man in his likeness, he mirrored himself in this newly created being; he wanted to see what was missing in his being. When he observed Adam to be lonely in paradise in spite of all that was given to him for dominion, God realized man needed a companion—just like he did.

In putting Adam in a deep sleep, aside from doing a major body repair on him, God also intended that Adam would wonder when he woke up who this new creature was—like giving the elements of surprise and wonder, a short drama of "wow" and "woo". Why did God make Eve's physical features—rounded boobs, small waistline, curved hips, pretty face, smooth thighs and legs—different from Adam's? Did God intend that Eve should look desirable to Adam? Or was Eve the reality of what God wished to behold? In making Adam in his likeness, how Adam reacted to the sight of Eve, is just the same as how he would react if Eve were his companion. Did Adam know that this new creature was taken from his rib? In Genesis 2:23, Adam said, "This one at last is bone of my bone and flesh of my flesh; this one will be called 'woman' for from him she was taken." In this statement Adam acknowledged that this creature he called "woman" is an integral part of his being. He knew she was made out of his ribs. This is the reason why a man leaves his father and mother and clings to his wife (Gen. 2:24). The pair now becomes one flesh, as in married to each other, thus being viewed as one being before the eyes of the Creator.

Nowhere in the Bible could we find a line or a verse that would tell us why God has to create by pairs in the lower forms of animals and two individuals in human beings, and then called them male and female. On what criteria can we call this being a male and also a female? If God created man in his image and likeness and taking into account the masculine attributes of God that Jack Miles enumerated; Adam being the first man he thus created, where did the female attributes of Eve come from? In the audiotape *Conversation with God; an uncommon dialogue (Neale Donald Walsch, 1996)*, God is the "great is not is; the am not am" or a dichotomous being, having dual characteristics. The attributes of Adam as a male and the attributes of Eve as a female are derived from one source who is God. In this context man and woman are inseparable as they are a manifestation of Gods very own nature; the male attributes as the "is" and the female attributes the "is not" or the other way around, like "darkness is the absence of light and that light is the absence of darkness". Or "good is the absence of evil, and evil is the absence of good". In Adam and Eve there were two separate bodies but one soul in the eyes of God. The "oneness" of Adam and Eve in the sight of God is a delight for God for he saw in them the completeness of his being. With his blessing and unconditional love, henceforth, Adam and Eve and their future generation shall be gathered in his kingdom to enjoy the bounty of endless bliss.

Although biology tells us that we both have the male and female chromosomes in our body, the dominant biological, physiological, and psychological characteristic defines our being. We cannot overlook the fact that there are individuals we call gays who manifest mixed and extraordinary characteristics. There are only two sexes—the male and female; homosexuality is not a kind of sexuality. Homosexuals are male or female who are attracted to and fall in love with individuals of the same sex—opposite to heterosexual where the attraction is with the opposite sex. Now that a number of gays and lesbians coming out from their closet have asserted equal recognition in society to be granted equal rights and privileges in marital laws, both civil and church, a number of states are legalizing same-sex civil marriages. Churches argued and debated whether to grant the same rights and privileges to their same-sex churchgoers. The questions that churches asked is: Isn't civil marriage enough for them to be together? Why insist on a church wedding? In biblical times marriages were all between a male and a female; God's intention was clear from the beginning: God created man in his image; male and female he created them (Genesis 1:27).

What has sex got to do with God? During the agonistic period, long before Christianity was born, humans believed that God is pleased to receive an offering that is of sexual nature. Tribal belief looked at God as a male being who preferred a beautiful virgin to be offered as a sacrifice to appease his anger. In some tribes, they danced around their God doing sexual intercourse to petition for fertility, that their God would bestow on the couples the seed for an offspring. Barren women would dance naked before their God to supplicate mercy and allow her to bear children.

The Church, in her teaching, always tells their members to view sex as a beautiful gift given from God for mankind to enjoy. The purpose of which God created two sexes—the male and female—is to procreate and dominate the world. In the act of procreating, God made it clear before Abraham, in a covenant by circumcision and in the wedding at Cana, in the miracle of the wine made by his son Jesus Christ, that the male and female must be wed into one flesh and model their love for each other the way God has loved them—that is, unconditional and outreaching. Yet mankind still, in their stubbornness, abuses and misuses their sexuality in many different forms, manners, and expressions. The irony, though, is when these abuses and misuses backfire; on bended knees mankind begs for forgiveness. Why is mankind stubborn when it comes to the affairs of the flesh? Is this because sex is just so compelling that to live without it is just like missing one big opportunity to experience "heaven"?

Sex in the Bible

I grew up seeing my father always seated on his favorite chair, reading the Holy Bible early morning and before sleeping. Being a "papa's girl," I did not have problem interrupting him in his readings. I would ask him questions about every thing, including what he was reading and how he would interpret them. He said the Holy Bible could not be easily understood in its true intention without the indwelling of the Holy Spirit. My father was a member of the Catholic Truth Defender in our parish. They'd go to places to debate and to defend the Catholic faith against other groups who were also travelling to propagate their beliefs. He said the first group of Bible scholars and interpreters used euphemism in their interpretation of the texts from the original language to what we have now. It was from him that I learned there were other interpretations of the story of creation, particularly the temptation story of Adam and Eve.

The Bible scholars of old knew that sex was, is, and will always be a hot subject to talk about; and to avoid being misunderstood as condoning it, they use ordinary words to replace the real text as originally written. In one of the many encounters my father experienced with other religious groups, the topic about the temptation of Adam and Eve was the most controversial and difficult to argue about because the story involved the sexuality of Adam and Eve and God's role in their life thereafter. One group said that the tree of knowledge of good and evil actually did not exist. The words "tree of knowledge of good and evil" were used to replace the "penis and the testicles" of Adam, and the word "apples" replaced the "breasts" of Eve. The words "in the middle of the Garden of Eden where the tree of knowledge of good and evil was" meant in the middle of Adam's body, where his penis and testicles were. The "Garden of Eden" is a euphemism of Adam's body. Garden in ordinary concept is a place where seeds sprout into plants; into trees. Adam's garden carried the seed that becomes another being—his offspring. The devil told Eve to touch the tree and eat the fruit (the first oral sex), and Adam was aroused. He also touched and ate the "apples" of Eve, and she was also aroused. Another group contended that there was a real tree of knowledge of good and evil, but the devil misled Eve by telling her that the tree that God meant was their own body and that if they'd touch each other's body parts, they would find heaven and they would be like God. Some Bible readers asserted that there were actually two trees God was telling Adam and Eve: one, the tree of knowledge of good and evil, said to be a symbolism of the physical body of Adam and Eve; and two, the tree of life, a symbolism of the spiritual aspect of their being, which after the fall of Adam and Eve were guarded by the cherubim and the fiery revolving sword. Others insisted that the tree of knowledge of good and evil and the tree of life were the same. My father further added that everywhere in the Holy Bible were stories about sex and God; that sex was created by a loving god for mankind to enjoy and appreciate. It was the devil's version of sex, which was lust that made mankind sinful—how we use and abuse it. The sex lives of those biblical men and women could not be ignored because sex formed an integral part in their lives and how God played an active role in that aspect as well.

In the story of Noah and his ark, God saw that the sons of heavens saw how beautiful the daughters of man were, and so they took them for their wives. The sons of heavens had intercourse with the daughters of man, who bore sons called the *Nephilim*. They were the heroes of old, the men of renown. God did not want the heavenly creatures to have sex with the mortals that he decided to wipe out his creations, except Noah and his family who found favor with the Lord. After the deluge, Noah and his family started a new generation of men. Although the Holy Bible did not imply what Noah's son Ham did to him upon seeing him naked while being drunk, we can tell the offense was grave to be worthy of Ham's future generation to be committed to slavery. Other Bible interpreter thinks that Ham, aroused by the nakedness of his father, sexually assaulted the drunken man, Ham being the first homosexual.

When Abraham went to Egypt, he instructed his wife Sarai to pretend she was his sister so his life would be spared, but the Pharaoh took Sarai for his wife, only to be returned to him when God struck the Pharaoh and his household with severe plagues (Gen. 12:10-20). God also intervened in the pregnancy of Hagar and Sarah and blest their circumcised sons, Ishmael and Isaac. God made a covenant with Abraham by requiring all descendants of Abraham to be circumcised. Jack Miles, in his *God: A Biography*, explains how important circumcision to God was: it symbolizes God's active participation in the sexual activity of all of Abraham's descendants. The destruction of *Sodom* and *Gomorrah* by pillars of fire, which happened during the time of Abraham, was also about the sexual abomination of the people in that city. In the story he sent two angels to convince Lot and his family to leave the city; but the people, upon learning of Lot's two visitors, sexually assaulted the angels. This angered God. After escaping from the fires of *Sodom* and *Gomorrah*, Lot's two daughters made him drunk and had sexual intercourse with him.

In the story of Jacob, Isaac's youngest son, rivalry between his two wives, Leah and Rachel, as to who could give him children, extended to their respective maids. All four women gave Jacob thirteen children—one daughter and twelve sons; one of them was Joseph who was commissioned by the Pharaoh to oversee the land of Egypt when he made the right interpretation of the Pharaoh's dream. The story of Joseph's fate in Egypt included, among others, a sexual seduction by his master's wife, which landed him in jail because, desperate and embarrass of her plot, she made up a lie against Joseph (Gen. 39:7-20). Dinah, Jacob's daughter by Leah, was defiled by Shechem son of Hamor the Hevite. Shechem was so in love with her and was willing to marry her. One of the conditions for marriage was circumcision of all males in Hamor's community, including Shechem; but Simeon and Levi, the full brothers of Dinah, slaughtered Shechem and his father, even though they agreed with the circumcision (Gen. 34:1-30). In Genesis 35:22, Reuben, Jacob's son by Leah, had sex with Bilhah, the maid of Rachel with whom Jacob had two sons—Dan and Napthali.

In Genesis 38:6-10, Onan, Judah's son, was told by his father to give his brother's widow an heir; he did sleep with his brother's wife and have sexual intercourse, but he withdrew before ejaculation and spilled his seeds on the ground instead so that he could not impregnate his brother's widow. Onan was killed because the Lord God was displeased with what he did. In continuation of the story, Tamar, the widow of Onan's brother Er, posed as a prostitute and had sexual intercourse with Judah, her father-in-law, with whom she bore twin boys. Upon learning of what she did, Judah ordered her to be burnt as a punishment.

In Moses's time, Aaron, his assistant who accompanied him to see the Pharaoh of Egypt for the release of the Israelite slaves, made a golden calf, while Moses was at Mt. Sinai receiving God's Ten Commandments, and told the freed Israelites to go naked and danced around the golden calf. Aroused and intoxicated, the Israelite performed sex in front of the golden calf. This angered Moses when he came down from the mountain and saw their abominations.

In Leviticus, God commanded Moses to speak to the Israelites to keep his decrees and statutes on *uncleanness of childbirth* (12:1-8), *personal uncleanness* (15:1-33), *the sanctity of sex* (18:1-30), and *the penalties for various sins* (20:1-27). In Deuteronomy chapters 21, 22, 23, and 24, God spoke of situations that has dos and don'ts about relationship, sex, and marriage. The story of Samson, his birth, marriage, and how he desired for Delilah that caused him his downfall, was narrated in Judges chapters 13, 14, 15, and 16. Ruth's mother-in-law, Naomi, advised her how to seduce Boaz, who in turn responded to her advances. She then became his wife, and they bore a son (the book of Ruth). There was also some sexual tone in the story of King David in 1 Samuel, 2 Samuel, and 1 Kings—how David's son Amnon desired for his sister Tamar, how he raped her, then sent her away after realizing his desire was only for lust. The story of King Solomon having three hundred concubines and seven hundred wives was told in 1 Kings 11:1-9, as *the sins of Solomon*, "The Song of Solomon," known as the "Song of Songs," contains sexual description on the relationship between the bride and the groom. This chapter contains in poetic form portrayal of an ideal human love as based on the love of God, the groom, and his people, the bride. Esther, the only woman among the virgins who pleased King Xerxes of Persia, saved the Jewish people from destruction (the book of Esther). Did King Xerxes find erotic pleasure "to the max" with Esther that he gave in to her plea to save her people from destruction? Isaiah had sex with a prophetess who conceived and bore a son (Isaiah 8:3). In Jeremiah, Lamentations, and Ezekiel, God compared Jerusalem's sinful ways to a harlot. Ezekiel 23:1-49 wrote about two sisters, Oholah, the personification of Samaria; and Oholibah, as Jerusalem, who had sex with the Egyptians and were punished by God. Hosea was ordered by God to marry a prostitute so that the children she would have would not be unmistakably his. She bore him three children, all of whom were given symbolic names. God accepted the third child Lo-ammi, meaning "not my people" (Hosea 1:1-8).

In the New Testament, Jesus Christ's first miracle was the transformation of water into wine in a wedding banquet. His presence and his mother's were significant as it showed that without God's participation in a marriage ceremony, the wedded couple could just end up running short of wine, the symbol of merriment and excitement; but with God invited in the wedding feast, the wine being served was the best and filled everyone present in the occasion. In Revelation chapters 2, 14, 17, 18, and 19, seduction, fornication, and adultery corrupting the earth are called abominations before God. In the New Testament, Jesus said that he came not to condemn the world but that the world might be saved through him. Jesus Christ was asked about adultery, celibacy, divorce, fornications, and marriage. His one answer was that all these are affairs of the flesh and that to have eternal life in God's kingdom, man has to repent and be born again in the spirit. In John 8:1-11, an adulteress named Mary Magdalene was brought before Jesus Christ for judgment. Jesus Christ did not condemn her but told her to repent and to sin no more.

Taking the Holy Bible as authored by God and knowing its contents, including sex, as sacred, inspired by the Holy Spirit, why do we look at sex as dirty and sinful? Why did the biblical writers, said to be inspired by God, include sex in their telling of the lives of those biblical people? What is the message? What measures morality? In the words of Pope John Paul II (Theology of the Body) God is the center of our sexuality, and relation of the sexes is the fiber of human existence. In the Old Testament, we can identify how those chosen people use and abuse sex and how God was pleased and displeased by their actions. The sexual account of the lives of those biblical people serves as a reminder to all faithful that sexual misuse and abuse are despicable before the eyes of God and, therefore, are punishable. Note here that post biblical event also happened in the city of *Pompeii*, where God destroyed the city in a volcanic eruption, which is "fire" in the form of molten lava, covering the entire city. In Pompeii the male phallus was considered sacred and revered by the people. When the archaeologist made a digging on the ashes of the place believed to be Pompeii, they found charred bodies of men and women still connected sexually to each other. In the *Siege of Waco*, aside from stocking ammunitions in preparation for his concept of Armageddon, David Koresh, the leader of a religious cult, had sexual contact with his female members as young as nine years old. The compound was engulfed with fire that killed the cult leader and all his members.

There are times in our lives that we experience catastrophes and misfortunes, which if we view them biblically, may have sent us a message that somewhere in our lives we did something despicable to God. In the Bible, hypocrisy and sexual abuses were the two human acts that anger God. In the times of Noah, in the times of Abraham, in the times of Moses, in the times of Onan, and in the times of Samson, God was angered.

Sex and Religion

Religion is a worship given to god, idols and false deities and in modern times to charismatic leaders. It is formed to answer man's quests for his identity and the reason why he exists. His search for answers connects him to the universe, in the space he occupies and to the other human beings and other creatures he sees around him. His quests make him believe in the existence of a supreme being that created all things including him. If a religion is formed with the objective or intention of following or believing a god, a deity, or a good leader, one of its tenets to be observed and followed by the members is on morality or spirituality. Since a human being is a composite of a body and a soul, morality aims at behaving in manners that are within social acceptance and with the purpose of nourishing the spirit in order to attain eternal life or immortality. As it is said that the body corrupts the soul (spirit) man must safeguard his physical behavior. There are other questions religion needs to address, like why is sex so compelling? Is Sex a sin? If it is a sin, what makes it a sin and how could man avoid committing this sin? Why pre-marital sex, polygamy, masturbation, homosexuality, and even rape are sins in some religion while in others they are not? Why in some religions, women are regarded as objects of pleasure only for men, while in other, women are considered one with man in marriage and must be treated with respect and with dignity.

With the guise of servicing the community and worshipping God, some religions are formed with hidden agenda such as for financial gains, power, influence, sexual privilege, and many other unspoken, unwritten reasons. Many religions accumulate wealth with their leaders enjoying luxury cars, fabulous mansions, and extensive travels around the world. Others, particularly those labeled as cults are organized to feed the sex appetites of their leaders. Others, to have political influence and control of people's right in government. This explains why up to this present times, religions are never united into one system of belief and objectives because some religious agenda contradicts in some ways.

Though the three major religions: Judaism, Christianity, and Islam believe in one God, they have differences and similarities in their teachings. Judaism differs from Christianity in their interpretations of the story of Adam and Eve. For the Jews the sins of Adam and Eve are mere disobedience of God's commandment, while in Christianity the concept of "original sin" is handed down to the future generations of Adam and Eve but were promised redemption and resurrection with the coming of a Messiah who will offer his life for the forgiveness of sins. To the Jews, the Song of Songs refers to the relationship between God, the groom and Israel, the bride. In Christian context it tells of the love of Jesus Christ, the groom to his bride, his church. Christianity puts so much importance on the sanctity of marriage—being the first sacrament instituted by Jesus Christ during a wedding at Cana. Celibacy and chastity are the virtues expected from individuals who choose to follow Jesus Christ in his ministry. On issues of human sexuality, Pope John Paul II addressed this in his lectures in *Theology of the Body*, expounded by Christopher West in his video and audiotape lectures.

Sexuality in Judaism has similarities in Buddhism in that sex is just like eating and drinking. Food nourishes the body, while sex nourishes the soul if done the right way and within acceptable conduct of behavior. Judaism takes marriage as the essential means to companionship, intimacy, and love. To be a holy person in Judaism, one has to be married and a second wife has to be selected for him because his service in the Temple would become invalid if the first wife dies and there is no replacement. Judaism maintains marital sex as the only relationship that provides emotional, spiritual, and physical fulfillment. Judaism, and Islam have similarities in their views of sex while the woman is having a menstruation. They consider the woman to be impure at this moment and therefore should not have sexual contact with a man. Sexual issues split Judaism in many small groups because others adhere to the strict discipline of their faith, while others adapt to the demands of modern times. Like in homosexuality, there are Jewish groups that tolerate and perform same sex marriages, while the conservative groups reject the idea.

In Islam, sex is considered a taboo. Virginity is the most guarded virtue a Muslim woman must keep. The rationale behind the covering of their entire body with *hijab* or *khimar* or *barqa*, which all means "cover", is to shield women from becoming object of lust in men. While sex is a privilege for men and those women are the source of their pleasure, Islam only allows men to have sex with their wives. Polygamy is legal as long as the man can afford to support his families. Having sex with an unmarried woman is punishable by law, but the irony of the law is that it is the woman being punished for allowing the man to touch her. Islam is silent on issues of homosexuality, lesbianism, prostitution, pornography, and all other forms of sexual perversion but if any one is caught engaging in such act, they are being punished by public stoning. Western observers noted some kind of flaws in the Islamic laws with regard to sexual crimes. In rape, being one of the crimes, punishment is imposed on the woman and not on the men that raped her. Virginity is required of a woman before marriage, but prostitution has been tolerated among girls as young as nine years old. If the scandal does not catch public attention, sexual criminals just get away with their crimes, but when someone complains and their crimes become public, punishment is so harsh like killing the parties—the victim and the victimizer—usually done by family members because such incident shames their families. One of the sacred books of the Islam faith is the *ahadith* which according to Abul Kasem, *Sex and Sexuality in Islam* is similar to *Kama Sutra*. It contains dos and don'ts in sex that every Muslim man must follow. The issue of having sex with seventy-two virgins as a reward to those men you give their lives to Allah became the subject of ridicule.

Baha'i, a religion that has many similarities with Islam and founded by Baha'u'llah has about 7 million followers all over the world. Its origin is said to be a "Persian" religion and their sacred text links to "Persian" culture. The "Aqdas" and its supplement, Questions and Answers treat three aspects of human sexuality which are sexual fluids, illicit sexual conducts and marriage. Sexual fluids like the semen and menstruation are considered ritual pollution, however innovation as to the treatment of these fluids as pollutant has been considered thus now these are treated as a matter of hygiene. Illicit sexuality—zina and liwat—and marriage also occupy a thorough discussion and explanation in their sacred text the Kitab-I Aqdas. Issues on homosexuality, pre-marital sex and sex outside of marriage are also addressed in this sacred text.

Many Westerners mistook Kama Sutra as part of Hinduism. Kama Sutra or rules of love is merely an impartial and systematic study of the essential aspects of existence, which one of them is human sexuality. All sexual variations—homosexuality, lesbianism, group sex and including relations with animals, which are seen in the facades of great temples, are mentioned in this complied book. Kama Sutra aims at the attainment of sexual pleasures at its highest level of satisfaction. Similar to a Christian concept, Hinduism, a predominant religion in India, considers the human body as a temple of the divine. Contemplative or meditative discipline is practiced to cleanse the body from its impurities and negative aspects and not to develop an attachment to it. Control of the body, the mind, and the senses is advocated in order to turn ones attention to ones inner self and his divine nature. Hinduism is misunderstood in the Western world as a mix voodoo and pornography in a sense that in their sacred books their gods are depicted as having some sexual activities. Erotic imagery of their gods could be seen in most Hindu temples. Because their gods change sexes, Hinduism believes that they are both male and female. Because tolerance is the essence of Hinduism since it does not oppose homosexuality, prostitution, and other forms of promiscuity; it is against sensual pleasures that degrade man and put his salvation at stake. The main focus of Hinduism is compassion and the adherent ability to see life in larger perspective. They show compassion to those ignorant souls who are victims of their own karma and whose lives are guided by their undisciplined human desires and weak aspirations. Hinduism believes in the reincarnation of the souls and it is up to man to discipline him in order to attain the highest level of enlightenment which is the "Nirvana".

Buddhism does not address sexuality in its teaching, but it is more focus on the discipline for the attainment of the highest level of enlightenment or consciousness called "nirvana" similar to the concept in Hinduism. Buddha teaches that if sex causes man some discomfort and unhappiness, he must detach himself from it. The main precept of Buddhism is to detach oneself from cravings of all earthly or materials pleasures. Any thing that causes man unhappiness, discomfort, guilt, shame and uneasiness, he has to control himself in order to reach full enlightenment. If an individual decides to become a monk or a nun, he/she has to observe complete sexual continence. Performing sexual intercourse in any form expelled him/her from the Order and is no longer in communion with the other monks. Marriage in Buddhism is not a sacrament and it is not the function of the monks to join two people in marriage. They could give a "blessing" after the civil wedding ceremony has been performed. Divorce, on the other hand, is also considered a civil affair. Buddhism does not believe that the world is created and ruled by God, but it believes in the law of cause and effect. It believes that the soul reincarnates in several ways until it reaches the highest level of enlightenment—a complete detachment from cravings or desires. Sex is not a sin in Buddhism. If one makes mistakes, including weaknesses of the flesh, one just recognize the mistake and avoid repeating such mistake and should not develop guilt-complex about them.

Taoism is the belief in achieving the ultimate reality which is the "Tao". Tao is the presence that existed before the universe was formed. It continues to guide the world and everything in it. Tao is not a god or supreme being but it is identified as the mother, or the source of all things. Taoism believes that by divesting oneself of all external distractions and desires, only then can one achieve Tao. With regard to man's sexuality, Taoism embraces or practices a form of discipline called "Jing chi", more or less similar to Buddhism in some aspects. *HeQi,* or *Jing Chi,* meaning *"Joining energy"* aims to conserve the male fluid by controlling ejaculation. The male which has the "yang" and the female which has the "yin" connects physically but instead of releasing the semen through ejaculation, it is controlled with the intention of keeping it and using it within the body for healing and spiritual growth. Sexuality in Taoism is not just for pleasing the man; the woman also had to be stimulated and pleased in order to benefit from the union or sex act. If a woman is stimulated and pleased she could create more jing, and the man could easily absorb the jing to increase his own jing.

Tantra, a form of sexual ritual which is focused on harnessing sexual energy to achieve union with the divine, is practiced both in India and in China. The Western world, particularly the New Age Group embraces and even modified the practice to fit their needs. It is similar to *HeQi* as it aims to conserve the male fluid by controlling ejaculation. In Tantra, the objective is to control physical orgasm and transform it to a spiritual orgasm, thus one experiences the so called "spiritual sex." In order to attain union with the universe and with the divine, one must learn complete control of self and all the other forces of nature. In Tantra, a sexual partner is not a must, since this could be practiced either alone or with a group.

There is less to be known about how Scientology viewed human sexuality because their founder L. Ron Hubbard considered pain and sex as the mere invention of the phychiatrist whose intention is to shrink people and cut their alertness, knowingness, power, and reach. Scientologist are warned not to engage in sexual activity during pregnancy because it is believed that it can have adverse and dangerous effect on the unborn child. This belief forms as the basis of Hubbard's "Silent birth" doctrine. The rationale behind this belief is that babies should not hear negativity that could damage their "prenatal" memory and could cause "psychic scars." It is also advised that couples must be silent while they copulate. Homosexuality is considered an illness or sexual perversion and promiscuity carries heavy penalties and punishments.

Almost all religions opposes pre-marital sex, infidelity, prostitution, homosexuality, pornography, and all forms of perversions, but with modern times demanding freedom of sexual expression, some religious groups break away from their main religion to accommodate members who are in these situations. Disciplining one's sexual appetite is a personal problem regardless of religion. Theologians and other religious leaders find it a problem since time immemorial to demand from their member's sexual purity or at least sexual righteousness. All religious congregations have in their membership some individuals with issues on their sexuality, and the best advice that they could offer is to pray for guidance.

Our life on earth is a journey, and religion provides us the vehicle to travel from our earthly existence to a place which is called in many names as Heaven, Paradise, Kingdom of God, Eternity, Endless Bliss, and Eternal Light. In whatever form of discipline we use to achieve immortality or to reach our final destination, our own sexuality is the most difficult to cultivate or to control. As long as man is alive, he will always desire for a woman, and the answer to his question why he does so, is embedded in the very fiber of his own existence.

Sex and the Religious Life

Every time our parish priest made an announcement that a group of seminarians would sing for the coming Sunday masses, every young girl in town got excited over the news. The girls would pick up their best clothes to wear during the occasion and would see to it that they got a seat near the choir stand. After the services, the girls flirted with the seminarians who were just as excited to meet them. Who would not be lucky to get a man from a group of would-be priest? They were an embodiment of good looks and intelligence while possessing such virtues as conservative, courteous, generous, God-fearing, honest, and patient. During the weekend that the seminarians were in town, the faces of these young ladies looked happy and hopeful. They hang around in the convent after the masses, volunteering any ministerial activities just to be within reach to the would-be priests, trying to get to know their names as well. I was one of them.

I befriended a number of women who now live with priests as married couples. When asked what attracted them to a priest for a husband, their answers were similar in many aspects, their virtuous character: honest, polite, religious, simple, loving, and the list of good adjectives goes on and on — the same characteristics that young girls saw in the young seminarians. They may know this kind of husband is not easy to find in the real world, but who would love to marry a mean-spirited male, anyway? Priests, the servants of God as they are oftentimes called, though are forbidden by the church to marry, fit the picture frame of an ideal husband; who knows one of them would change his heart. My widowed sister's second husband is an ex-priest.

In a situation where we find a priest leaving his priestly function for a woman, so many questions would be asked about them. What cause this to happen? Was it the woman's initiative or the priest's? Did the woman seduce the priest with her sexual innuendos? Did she make herself available to his needs because she wants him to be her husband? Does the priest know that leaving his priestly function in exchange for sexual gratification would expose him to the trials and tribulations of being a family man, or is he ready to face the challenges of a secular life for love's sake? How would he provide his new family when all along he has no means to do so, owing to the fact that his money allowance comes from the congregation and that the church funds solely come from the generosity of the parishioners?

Many of the couples I know experienced financial problems. They could hardly make both ends meet. In desperation they just accepted their hardship as a curse from God. Perhaps the very virtues that the priest possesses make him less competitive in the material world. His conscience would tell him not to cheat, not to exploit, not to scam, not steal, not to lie, not to compete, and not to make a huge profit if he is in business. These are good virtues, which the material world labels as weaknesses. Only few priests could survive in a dog-eat-dog society. Having stayed for many years in the seminary and in the parishes, they would have difficulty shoving these virtues aside. I ask a very close friend who is a priest what really makes a priest leave his priestly function? Is it sex or boredom from carrying the burden of his parishioners? What if the temptation of the flesh is so compelling? What should a seminarian or a priest do? He said the Catholic Church has been aware of this kind of problem ever since, and before a seminarian decides to profess celibacy, he has to accept the discipline the Church expects of him. He said prayer is a very powerful discipline to resist the temptation of the flesh. In moments where temptation of the flesh is so strong, either alone or with a woman, the priest with all his training and discipline from the seminary can resist such. "What kind of prayer would that be?" I asked. He answered, "The priest has to get away from the source of his temptation, either his thoughts or a woman. Then go to a private place and pray. Pray with intense meditation. When praying, the soul overpowers the flesh and weakens all his five senses.

In a very intense prayer, the priest will experience lightness of his body, as if levitating or floating from the ground. This experience of complete tranquility is likened to having a spiritual orgasm. When he comes back to his normal state, the desire of the flesh is completely removed. The saints know how it is. We have heard of so many mystics and religious people levitating during an intense prayer." I made a follow-up question, "What if the desires overpower this discipline?" He answered, "Only God knows what he will do, and God will understand." I asked further, "For how long God would keep on understanding him?" This was his reply: "God is never tired of us. He is a patient and a forgiving god." As I ponder upon his explanation, I seem to liken this to "Tantra", a sexual discipline that enables one to shift sexual energies to a higher level of spiritual bliss, avoiding orgasm. Siddhartha Gautama a young prince, who lived a lustful life and the founder of Buddhism, sat under a "Bodhi tree" in a very deep meditation to reroute his worldly thoughts to asceticism.

The encyclical "Sacerdotalis Caelibatus" issued by Pope Paul VI in 1967 synthesizes the profound theological reasons supporting the discipline of celibacy. First and foremost and following the life of Christ, the priest, who dedicated himself totally to the service of God and men as a mediator between God and the human race, shares and gives himself in the dignity and mission of Christ. Second, in order to draw supernatural vigor of spiritual fruitfulness between Christ and his spouse, which is the church, the sacred ministers themselves manifest the virginal love of Christ for the church by choosing celibacy. Finally in Matthew 22:30, Jesus Christ was asked about marriage and resurrection, taking the story of a widow who married all seven brothers and whose wife would she be. Jesus Christ told the Sadducees that none of the seven brothers are considered her husband because there is no marriage in heaven, and everyone would be like angels in heaven. In this context, marriage although considered a sacrament is not compulsory for salvation. Priestly celibacy proclaims the coming of a new dawn of salvation and can look forward to the promise of resurrection to all children of God (Pope John Paul II, Rise, Let Us Be on Our Way, 141-142).

Celibacy has its origin from the apostles. Although it was not sure if the apostles chosen by Christ had wives, except Peter who was said to have left his wife when he gave up his nets and his boat, the fathers of the Church were unanimous in declaring that those who might have been married gave up their marital lives and practiced perfect continence—meaning they terminated their sexual contact with their wives. In the book *The Apostolic Origins of Priestly Celibacy*, Christian Cochini, SJ, wrote stories about married deacons, married priests, married bishops (these men had wives when they chose to serve God) giving up their wives. They had but one theme in common: renounced the pleasure of the flesh and professed continence for the service of the Lord for they could not serve two masters at the same time: the Lord and pleasure. Martyrdom was also cited as another factor. During the early years of Christianity, the followers of Christ were being persecuted; the Church had to consider the parents, wives, and children left behind by them. It was then necessary and appropriate that those who chose to serve the Lord must sever their ties with their parents, wives, and children, thus making them free to offer their lives to God. Priestly celibacy had also its roots to the tribe of Levi in the Old Testament. The Levites were the descendants of the tribe of Levi, the third son of Jacob and Leah. They were given the mission of servicing the sanctuary and later on the tabernacle. They did not own properties or lands, and their sustenance was shouldered by the community through tithing. They did not have a family and were free to move to serve the different tribes in their worship of God. The book of Leviticus in the Holy Bible accounts the lives of the tribe of Levi and how priestly functions started. The main divisions of Leviticus are: I, *ritual of sacrifices* (Lv 1-7); II, *ceremony of ordination* (Lv 8-10); III, *laws regarding legal purity* (Lv 11-16); IV, *code of legal holiness* (Lv 17-26); and V, *redemption of offerings* (Lv 27).

The problem of the Catholic Church is not only about priests leaving their vows. There are issues such as homosexuality and child abuse or what is called "pedophile priests." Aware of the psychological problem homosexuals have with regard to their sexual needs, the Catholic Church invites them to devote their lives to the service of God. In Matthew 19:10-12, Jesus Christ explained to his disciples that there are individuals who are incapable of marriage because they were born so; some were made so by others and others who renounced marriage for the sake of the kingdom of heaven. In this explanation Jesus agrees that celibacy is not for all but only for those to whom God has granted them. A number of these homosexuals made it to the priesthood, but when access to the secular world was made available through their priestly service to the community, the temptation of the flesh became their downfall. These homosexual priests still could not resist the temptation of the flesh. The access is so easy because the victims are innocent children who are vulnerable. Now the Catholic Church is in trouble with these priests. It is unfair, though, for the concerned victims to attack the Church in general because these homosexual activities are personal of the priests. When a doctor rapes a patient, should the victim blame the hospital? If a teacher seduced a student, should the victim blame the school? When complains about sexual abuses are made against a priest, before the higher authorities of the Church could help him, he is already exposed to the media for scrutiny. The setup of the Catholic hierarchy makes help comes too late to fix the situation. The most the Church official could do is to transfer the concerned priest to another parish. To name a few, John Geoghan, a Catholic priest, was accused of child molestation; an Australian bishop was also accused of engaging in a porn scandal in the seminary he was given charge; Marcial Maciel Degollado, founder of Legionaries of Christ, was also accused of homosexual relationship in the seminary he founded. There are priestly abuses that were not reported because the families involved just decided to either leave the parish or to move on with their lives as an obedient family of God.

Similar problems are also happening in other congregations, but because their population is manageable, their church leaders and elders are able to conceal them as quick as they could before the media gets hold of the issue. Evangelicals who are caught having sexual relationship with women not their wives are put on the line for scrutiny and judgment, sometimes being forced to go down from their pedestal of righteousness. Jimmy Swaggart of the Assemblies of God, Baton Rouge, Louisiana, had an affair with a prostitute (1988); Rev. Jesse Jackson, had a daughter outside of marriage; Jim Baker, Kim Bakker, 1970-1987, Ted Haggard of World Prayer Center, Colorado, Spring; The Second Prophet Brigham Young of the Mormons 1847-1877, had fifty wives and

South African President Jacob Suma, a religious leader, has several wives. Other abuses reported on religious leaders having a family are domestic violence and embezzlement of church funds.

Charismatic leaders, mostly religious people, used religion to fill in their sexual appetite; David Koresh (real name Vernon Howell), a religious leader, told his followers that God told him to father many children with the female members of his cult known as Branch Davidians situated at Waco Texas, including teenage girls and wives of other male members. While he enjoyed having sex with the female members, he obliged some male to remain celibate. In 1993, the government raided the compound on the ground that they had become a threat because they were stockpiling guns and ammunitions, which according to Koresh was in preparation for Armageddon.

Rev. Jim Jones (1957-1976), who founded the People's Temple in Indianapolis, moved to California, and then permanently to Guyana, used religion to satisfy his sexual appetite. He used sex not just for pleasure but for power. He claimed to have a superhuman potency, technique, and endurance that he even consulted a psychiatrist to advice him on how to control his libido. When some members begun defecting and when investigation of their activities was conducted, he convinced his followers to drink cyanide. When everyone was dead, Jones took a pistol and blew his brains out.

Adolfo de Jesus Constanzo, a Cuban cult leader, used sex to divide and rule his followers by sleeping with both sexes. He would conduct satanic rituals in their sexual orgies, using human as a sacrifice. Most of the victims were from the homosexual world of which he was a part. When the authorities discovered their secret activities, when cornered by the authorities in a gun battle, Constanzo ordered one of his members to shoot him and his companion.

The stories of David Koresh, Jim Jones, Adolfo de Jesus Constanzo, other cult and religious leaders, priests, and anyone in the religious vocations that were in trouble tell a belief common in all of them—that god does not condemn anyone who falls into sin because of one's sexual needs. In their thinking god merits their cause over their weaknesses of the flesh. When the affairs of the spirit mixed up with the affairs of the flesh, they put themselves in trouble. They misled their followers by twisting biblical passages to their benefit. "For those who live according to the flesh are concerned with the things of the flesh, but those who live according to the spirit are concerned with the things of the spirit. The concern of the flesh is death, but the concern of the spirit is life and peace" (Letter to the Romans 8:5-6).

We would be asking how Mother Teresa of Calcutta handled her sexual desires. She was human just like us, and naturally she would have the desire of the flesh once in a while in her lifetime. We would also be asking all those who choose to serve God as a priest or as a nun the same question. The answer could be found in that instance when they answered their calling—they offered themselves in marriage to their vocation as a service to God and his people. Mother Teresa's devotion and commitment to her marital vows were demonstrated in her sacrificial offering of love and service to the poorest of the poor. Erotic desires of individuals are inseparable to the love of God and the love of neighbors and those individuals who choose celibacy has to discipline their "Eros" and transform it into "agape" which is the love towards God and others, an ascending-descending kind of love (Pope Benedict XVI, Deus Caritas Est—God is Love),

By reading the stories of how the saints lived their lives, we can see the kind of focus and discipline they had when they choose to sacrifice their physical desires over their desire to serve God. While still on earth, they all underwent death of their pride, death of their material desires, death of their vices, and death of their self—all for the desire to have joy in the kingdom of God and enjoy the reward of having eternal life with their creator. To recall what Jesus Christ told Nicodemus: "unless you are born again in spirit, you will never see the kingdom of God." In the word of Saint Francis of Assisi, "It is in dying that we are born to eternal life."

God Is Love

For a lifetime we've been hearing this statement, "God is Love." Do we believe this? Should we believe this? With all the disasters and catastrophes happening in many places of the world and the many trials and tribulations of living, people begin questioning, "Where is God? Is this how God loves us?" Because no one can give us a definite answer to this question, we begin to doubt the existence of God and also the meaning of love. Religious leaders find it a duty to make the people hold on to their faith in spite of all these things happening to us. But with so many religious groups abounding everywhere, people get confused instead.

Do we see God's love in the rubbles of concrete caused by an earthquake trapping helpless people, in the murky waters of a flood washing away destroyed homes and lifeless bodies, in the piles of debris and dead bodies after a hurricane or a storm? Did we find God's love on September 11, 2001, when the two towers in New York collapsed with more than three thousand dead bodies buried in ashes? Do we see God's love in poverty-stricken countries with so many destitute families wanting of food and clothing? Everyone will say, "No. God was never there, because if he were there, those things would never have happened." We always wanted God to stop the workings of nature. When man altered nature; nature breaks, but when nature breaks because of our own doing, we blame God. If help does not come along, we doubt his existence. How about us? How do we love God in return? Those natural disasters and the inequities of the world are not measurements of God's love for us. In fact, it is the reverse. They are measurements of how much we love God. In those catastrophes, the dead are already in God's hand. Who takes care of the survivors who lost their loved ones, their dreams, their future, and their hopes? Should we tell God to take care of them too when we, the living, are reflections of God's love and compassion? When we offer our hands and show compassion to the survivors, there we are showing how much we love God. Jesus Christ said, "Whatever you do to the least of my brothers; you do it unto me."

Man's interaction with other creatures is guided by his intellect and his emotions. On the emotional side, man's longing to connect with another human being has its root from his creator. As a living being made on God's image and likeness, his desires reflect his creator's desire. While God made the insects, birds, beasts, and animals in pairs, he intentionally made man without a pair yet, in order for him to know what this creature would need if he was by himself. Being alone in a void, God wants to know through man what he desires: *he desires to love and be loved*; and so he created mankind. Before creating a woman, the Lord God said, "It is not good for man to be alone," so out of the ground he created various animals, insects, and flying creatures and give man the privilege to give a name on each of them, but none proved to be suitable partner for man. When he created man's companion, he added a little mystery to it by putting him into a deep sleep, then taking out one of his ribs, which he formed into a woman. That is why a man leaves his mother and father and clings to his wife. And the two of them become one body. Mankind, thus, become in the union of Adam and Eve (Gen. 2:18-24). (Although this statement did not apply to Adam because he did not have a father and a mother, the Bible scholars intended to address this statement to future man and woman relationship. It emphasizes the significance of man's commitment to his wife in a marital bond.)

To have a deeper understanding of how immense God's love for us is, let us go back to very source of the statement, "God is Love," which is the Holy Bible. God just can't forsake man. When he saw Adam and Eve wearing fig leaves, in spite of their disobedience, he made them leather garments to wear. When Cain was banished after killing Abel, he promised to Cain that whoever kills him will be avenged sevenfold. When he destroyed his people in a deluge, he saved Noah and his sons and provided them many things in order to survive. In his covenant with Abraham, he promised to bless his descendants, even the descendants of his illegitimate son Ishmael. He talked to Abraham and gave warnings before he decided to destroy Sodom and Gomorrah, sparing Lot and his family. He sent Moses to free the Israelites from slavery in Egypt. Even the Pharaoh, an obstinate man, was given ten chances to make up his mind when Moses and Aaron begged him to consider their request. He was with Joshua and his men in their battle to gain the Promised Land. He was in constant communication with the prophets, and to prove further how much he loves mankind, he gave his only beloved son to die for us so that everyone who believed in him might not perish but might have eternal life. God wants us all to be in his kingdom forever.

God's love for mankind is likened to the love of the groom to his bride. The "Song of Songs," said to be written by King Solomon, was interpreted by some Bible scholars and theologians as an allegory of God's love for the Israelites and, in the Christian teaching, as the relation of Jesus Christ and his church. The emphasis here is the *groom*, not the husband; and the *bride*, not the wife, for any man can become a husband and any woman a wife without the benefit of a sacramental blessing, as in a civil marriage. When a man proposes marriage to a woman, he made a commitment to love and to cherish, to have and to hold, for better and for worse, in sickness and in health. The terms "bride" and "groom" are used to designate the woman and the man in a wedding ceremony with the priest or religious authority performing the sacramental blessing. It is at this moment that God, the Father of us all, will bind them together until death do they part; and what God has joined together, let no man put them asunder.

It is a grave sacramental injustice for a husband to leave his family because of financial difficulty or when his child or his wife gets ill or become disable. It is also a grave sacramental injustice for a husband to use his wife's sexuality, calling her a slut, as a means to debase her in times of marital conflict. When a man abuses his wife emotionally, physically, and verbally, he breaks his marital vow to love and to cherish, to have and to hold, because the body of his wife, also considered the temple of God, is being made to suffer in pain. Domestic violence is an act of destroying not only the body, but also the soul. In this situation love is just nowhere in the relationship. The Church would even grant annulment on marriages that are extremely violent, like threatening the life of one partner. Life is at stake in a violent relationship.

Pope Benedict XVI wrote in his first encyclical letter entitled "DEUS CARITAS EST" (God is Love) the kind of love God has offered mankind. This letter to his flocks explains how fundamental God's love is for our lives and how it raises questions about who we are and who is God. He said love is a single reality but with different dimensions; at different times, one or other dimension may emerge more clearly. The dimensions are different in the sense that erotic love or "Eros," as an ascending, possessive, or covetous love, is non-Christian, this having derived from Greek culture; while "Agape" or descending love is Christian, yet these two can never be separated. When these two dimensions are cut off from one another, the result is an impoverished form of love. Christianity believes that man is a composite of two inseparable elements: the body and the soul—Eros being a physical love and Agape a spiritual. God's love is unconditional and forgiving as we see when he sent his beloved son Jesus Christ—*the incarnate love of God*—to die on the cross for us. In the words of Pope John Paul II, "God's love does not impose burdens upon man that he cannot carry, nor make demands that he cannot fulfill, for whatever God asks of man, God provides the help that is needed" (Rise, Let Us Be On Our Way, 215).

The Greek considered *Eros* as a "divine madness" that overpowers reason as it intoxicates man in his desire to experience supreme happiness (the ultimate bliss). According to this encyclical, *Eros* has to be disciplined and purified if it is to provide, not just fleeting pleasure, but a certain foretaste of our divine destiny to experience the beatitude which we all desire. Erotic love has its beginning in the Garden of Eden. God took a rib from Adam while he was asleep, and then made it into a woman. Man has to find that missing rib that he lost, so he seeks for it, and he sees a woman. At this point the union of the man and the woman demonstrated the physical aspect of love; Eros becomes merely a biological need. In the union of the flesh through the sacrament of marriage, Eros becomes concern with and caring of the other. It is no longer self-seeking intoxication of happiness; instead it seeks the good of the beloved and is even willing to suffer. Marriage based on love becomes the symbol of the relationship between God and his people.

In 1 Corinthians 13:4-13, love is defined as patient and kind. It is not rude or jealous. It does not harbor grudges, hate, or wrongdoings. Its concern is to make the other happy as it is considerate and never quick-tempered. It has no intent of causing emotional, physical, and spiritual injury to the other. Love is not inflated or pompous; it rejoices with truth and believes in all things. It can hope; it can endure because love never fails.

So moving is the power of love, that movies showing love in their themes draw large numbers of viewers wishing to connect their lives to the characters in the movies. Books of love and romance are always best sellers making readers skip sleep just to find how love touches the characters in the book as they touches theirs. Works of art like drawing, painting, and sculpting that depict the face of love are objects of possessions regardless of the price they demand. Dances also show graceful executions of steps that interpret the magnificence of love as it moves with the music. Man's deepest longing for love, the earnest desire to love and be loved by someone, is spoken in the anthologies of great song writers and poets. Our emotions overflow with immeasurable joy or sadness when reading those love poems or listening to those love songs. Yet with all of these, man still can't fathom the internal message of love; we find love a mystery that makes our souls restless. As St. Augustine, the greatest sinner and the greatest saint of the Catholic Church concluded, that after a lifelong quest for the answers to his restless soul, it only finds its rest in God – the god who loves unconditionally.

An unknown poet wrote his own definition of love this way: Love is friendship that has caught fire. It is quite understanding, mutual confidence, sharing and forgiving. It is loyalty through good and bad times. It settles for less than perfection and makes allowances for human weaknesses. Love is content with the present; it hopes for the future, and it doesn't brood over the past. It's a day-in and day-out chronicle of irritations, problems, compromises, small disappointments, big victories, and working toward common goals. If you have love in your life, it can make up for a great many things that are missing. If you don't have love in your life, no matter what else there is, it's not enough. The last two sentences in this definition explain to us why there are so many kings and queens who gave up their thrones for love and so many destitute couples who stay happy together in their daily struggles to survive because of love. It is love that unites their soul together.

A sexual desire use to express love connects man and woman into a relationship that goes beyond physical pleasure. It is the ultimate desire to make the other person attain full satisfaction, connecting not only their bodies but also their soul. The sexual acts exalt them into a higher level of excitement that seems ecstatic and heavenly. In this union, the only desire there is to give joy to the other. Love is the ultimate reality—the experience of God. What could be more divine than true love consummated in a sexual union? Lust being the devil's version of sex is an arduous desire to use the other person's body for personal gratification. It does not care what the other person feels. There is no sense of commitment after the act. There could be regret, anger, or even violence. Lustful sex wears out fast. It is like a house engulfed in flames that when the fire dies out, the house is gone and all that the owners of the house gather are the ashes of shame and regret. Suffering and sacrifices are like fire testing the purity of gold. At old age, the love, through day-to-day suffering and sacrifices, shared by the couples when they were young, makes their marriage stays like pure gold that has been tested by fire. The symbolism of wine at the wedding of Cana tells us that as wine aged, it tastes better and better through time. When two mortals are in love with each other, time is frozen; distance is non-existent. They breathe as one with the infinite. When two mortals commit their life for love, their hearts beat as one with the divine, the source of a love that is outreaching and unconditional. At old age, when their bodies can no longer perform the sexual act, love that was aged like wine keeps the couples together. True love as a reflection of God's love rests in perfect bliss with its creator.

Part V

*The Answer: The Seedbed
of Sexual Impulse*

By the sweat of your face

Shall you eat bread,

Till you return to the ground,

For out of it you were taken;

For you are dusts

And to dust shall you return.

—Genesis 3:19

The Ground

The English word "germ" carries two opposite definitions in the dictionary. When we say "to germinate," taken from the word "germ," we mean "to begin to grow or develop, to sprout." The first definition of the word "germ" (*botany*) is "the earliest form of an organism; a seed, bud, or spore; (*biology*) a. the formative protoplasm of an egg or ovum, or of an ovule; a gamete cell, b. the earliest stage of an organism." This definition connotes the beginning of life. The second definition is "a microorganism; especially, one likely to cause disease; a microbe" (Funk and Wagnalls 1987). Any living organism invaded by microbes that carry diseases begins to decay, and if uncontrolled, the organism dies, These two definitions imply the beginning and the end of life—a revelation of God who is the Alpha and the Omega. The four basic elements of nature—earth, fire, air, and water—are the essential factors that make a germ live or cause it to die. Connecting this fact to the story of creation (Gen. 1:9-12; 2:4-7) that God made all things from the ground, we can deduce a conclusion that the ground (clay) being fertile is where God embedded "life," a germ, a seed that can grow and develop with the ground. Since man and all the animals, insects, and beasts were made from the ground, they carried in their very nature the germ of fertility. With all the four elements working as one—the ground holding the germ, the heat coming from the sunlight, water from the rain, and all the gasses in the air—life begins; in the absence of any of these four elements, the germ decays, causes illness, and death happens.

The ground holds the secret of the physiological explanation of life. All living organisms grow and develop into new similar organisms to preserve and propagate the species. Any deviation from the natural order is said to have mutated, which is caused by some other radical elements in the process. Germs that are microbes and cause diseases are the very germs that cause growth but has gone awry because of other incompatible factors it contacted from the environment. Cancer cells could also be the normal germs of a living being that underwent radical metabolism caused by traumas, malnutrition, and stress. Diseases carried by germs are potent and alive that if they contact other living organisms would have an adverse result. Sexually transmitted diseases could be the gamete cells of an individual that has gone abnormal because of a contact with an incompatible cell. An example is the prostitute that receives several gamete cells from different men she has in sexual contact with; she acts as the receptacle or the mixing pot that kept the mismatched gametes. The mixture of several incompatible gamete cells mutates into microbes that then carry diseases such as syphilis, gonorrhea, and other diseases. In homosexual relationship, mutation might have occurred when a living potent cell is passed through the throat or through the anus and had contact with radical cells, then becoming the AIDS virus. Likewise, heterosexual relationship that also does oral and anal sex could also acquire AIDS. The natural formula for reproduction is the union of gamete cells, which are the egg of a female and the sperm of a male. Other than this, the gamete cells mutate and become destructive.

Science has all different theories regarding how life on earth started. Even at present times, debates continue as to which theory is scientifically true, logical, and acceptable. We heard and read about the evolution theory by Charles Darwin, how life-form on earth started. It is a study of how groups of already existing things change over time. While we have seen lower forms of creations evolving to another form of being, years have already passed by and humans are not found evolving into another higher being. Those who did not advocate such theory asked the questions how did humans acquire intelligence if their ancestors are the apes? Another theory "Abiogenesis" postulates that life started from inanimate matter. Most amino acids, often called "the building blocks of life," can form via natural chemical reactions unrelated to life. Stanley Miller and Harold Urey conducted an experiment to support the theory (http://en.wikipedia.org/wiki/Abiogenesis).

Two scientists from the University of Washington, John Baross and Mausmi Mehta, conducted a research on the single-celled organism collected from the ocean, off the Pacific Northwest coast. This single-celled organism known as archaea was believed to be the first form of life on the planet—at the Axial Volcano. They have this notion that life on Earth began within the deep dark ocean in the superheated seafloor environment of submarine volcanoes (http://www.seattlepi.com/national/296146_deepseabug16.html).

Plato explained a Greek myth that man was divided in two and how the two halves became man and woman. Since each of them is only a half, each forever seeks the other half (Ratzinger, 2002). A Filipino folklore has similar story as Plato's: a bamboo was split open by some nature's spark, and on each part came the first man named "Malakas," meaning strong; and the first woman named "Maganda," meaning beautiful. Tribal groups from all parts of the world have also their own stories of the beginning of life. Theologians and mystics, as well, have their own teaching and beliefs about the beginning of life on earth. Biblical account of the beginning of man is told in Genesis, the first book in the Old Testament.

In space exploration, NASA scientists' concern is to find life in the planet being explored. A planet found to have vegetation is considered livable because the ground is fertile and there is water—a compound of 2hydrogens and 1oxygen. NASA scientists' other concern is to study the temperature of the planets. Excessive or lack of heat and presence of gaseous elements in the planets determine a livable environment. Science fanatics also believe that the first people on earth were aliens. They adapted to the earthly elements and then became humans.

All plants, shrubs, and trees "germinate" from the ground and bear seed-bearing fruits; and all living creatures, insects, beasts, animals, and humans "copulate" to propagate life and preserve the species. Humans could be just like all other animals in their mode and style of copulation (we can name a few among our friends), but because God gave us a soul and made us a rational being, our sexuality has to be moderated within the limits of social and moral norms. Perverts use their sexuality to explore how far man as an animal can violate social and moral norms. Pedophiles use their childlike emotion to fill in the need for sexual gratification.

Pornographer and prostitutes use their body to provide financial security; homosexuals find love and sexual comfort with their own kind; serial killers and sex criminals equate sex with their longing to be loved, and married couples commit their sexual needs to each other in marriage vows.

When Jesus Christ was confronted by a mob that was chasing an adulteress by stoning her as she ran for her life, he stopped the crowd. He said that who among them has not sinned cast a stone on her; the crowd moved back and went away. They knew they were sinners too. Jesus asked the woman if there was one who condemned her, and she said no one. Jesus said neither did he. While talking to the crowd, Jesus was seen writing something with his finger on the ground (John 8:1-11). What was it that he wrote about? Was it in connection with the scenario of the day? Was he writing or just pointing his finger to the ground? Jesus Christ was not writing; he pointed his finger to the ground to remind the crowd what was written on Genesis 2:7: "God formed man out of the clay from the ground." This answers why sex is so compelling and why we cannot separate ourselves from it; the urge to copulate is embedded in our very own nature. The ground from which we were made is fertile, carrying the germ that could become another human being. The law of nature dictates that this germ has to grow and develop into another being. The human body will manifest this need; on the female she ovulates, and her body temperature raises; that is why she is said to be in "heat." On the male part, very obvious in the lower form of animals, he smells the heat emitted by the female, and then he responds to the female advances or flirtations. In humans, the male would know if the woman is in "heat" because she shows her unease with flirtations. While plants and all lower forms of animals follow the dictates of nature, humans has to follow, not only the law of nature, but also the law of moral and social conduct. This complicates man's role because there are times nature overrule reasons. People with mental disorder, though deprived of sound reasoning, still have the urge to copulate. It is their brain/mind that has impairments, but their bodies still follow the law of nature. The "urge" is just there, making them restless, wanting for a release. There is a difference between having an "urge" and having the "desire." Urge compels living creatures to copulate;

it is like having an itch that needs to be scratched. To desire is to express a physical need, an attraction, or an emotion, which can only be satisfied by having contact with or by having possession of the desired object. What is compelling is unavoidable, making one restless; what is beautiful is desirable, making one joyful. There is relief after the urge is served; there is joy after the desire is fulfilled.

Temporal Pleasures

During the time when I took a twenty-day vacation in my province, I oftentimes found myself alone in the hotel where I was staying, still awake until two o'clock in the morning. I would stand by the window and survey the serene panoramic view of the city with rows of lighted post and limited empty streets within my view; with only few cars running. I knew out there were people still awake at that time. Maybe inside some of the houses, people were making love; they could be a husband and a wife, a lover and a mistress, a prostitute and a customer, or gay lovers sharing passionate moments together. Maybe somewhere in the dark alleys of a narrow street, a pedophile lured an innocent child to his house; or somewhere in the unlighted remote corners of the city, a sex offender or sex criminal tortured his victim. The world has all people wanting of sex; some of them think that sex is an expression of love or that love can only be express through sex. We all agree that sex is a wonderful experience, and the pleasure we get doesn't last for long. After the first encounter, we still would wish and want for more. If there were ways of keeping it to last forever, we all would grab the opportunity at any cost.

We do any thing to make sex romantic—buy transparent negligees, seductive bras, and underwear of tempting colors. We rubbed perfumes and lotions to make our body attractive to the partner. We light candles to create a cozy and tantalizing environment; we dim the lights and play a romantic music to add a little mystery for the moment, but we could not do anything to make it everlasting; the pleasure we get just fleets away.

Once orgasm is reached and the fluids are then released, sex has done its part, and that's it. The steaming passion evaporates into thin air and disappears. Yet we still look for something more beyond sex. Married couples stay together in an embrace after the lovemaking, maybe talk about the wonderful experience they just had together or perhaps agree to do it again. The prostitute may experience a hug and kiss from her customer, but she can never give a loving response to a stranger whose name she doesn't even know and whose face she could not see again. The man on the other hand knows that this kind of passion is limited only to his carnal needs and nothing more. The pornographers somehow cannot find love with their sex partners. Once the video session is over, that's it: cut the act, pack their things, and go home. The rapist enjoys sex without the benefit of a loving response from his victim and probably realizes that after his act, he is still the lonely man in the neighborhood and will always be for the rest of his life. There is neither a hug nor an embrace during his act. And how could a pedophile get love from a child? How could an old man in a nursing home find love in the company of paid caregiver? He would only be wishing for the wife that he lost because of domestic violence, abuse, and indifference? Could these people ever find the answer to their longings?

Human beings have needs of all sorts, and one of those needs is the desire to be happy and find fulfillment in his being. Some find fulfillment in the wealth they have acquired, in the achievements and prestige they gain from their labor, in the families they have built and gathered, in the faith they have chosen to believe in. But all these have limitations. Our lives, our pleasures are but temporary; yet in the deepest part of our being we know there is something that stays permanent, something that makes us feel complete and at peace that when we found this something, we found rest; and we ask nothing more.

We can deduce from our knowledge in physics that matter, in this case the dust from which man is made of, is finite. Although matter can be transformed from one state to the other—into solid, liquid, gas, or plasma—the human body, which is in its solid state, becomes dust after death. Perhaps the gas in us escapes in the decay process, but there is something in us that doesn't decay nor die. It is called the soul. The soul is the one that seeks for its final rest in the afterlife. This soul hopes to be in union with its source—its creator.

To understand man as a form of matter leads us to the very root of our creation. In Genesis 2:7, God formed man out of the clay of the ground and blew the breath of life into his nostrils, and he became a living being. God made this being male and female and equipped them with reproductive tools, the sex organs that will enable them to multiply and dominate the earth. Man's body is governed by different systems that could sustain him to live a healthy and normal life. These systems follow the laws of nature.

Though man's reproductive system is created to produce and replenish seminal fluids necessary for erection and ejaculation under healthy and normal conditions, and the woman's to produce the eggs with the aid of a regular menstrual cycle, these are subjected to some limitations. Somehow the reproductive part of their bodies has to cease to function as dictated by their very nature—it could be old age, illness, or disability. The law of nature states that "all matters are finite," and the human body is no exception.

Our sexual capabilities can be explained in this simple analogy: The manufacturer made the electric bulb to have one thousand lumen hours. If we turn on the lights twenty-four hours a day, the bulb will no longer light up after forty-two days (1,000 /24 hours a day = 41.66 days). But if we turn on the lights for only five hours a day, it would last for two hundred days (1,000/5 hrs. /day = 200 days). Another analogy: With modern cars nowadays run by a preprogrammed microchip—say the chip can make the car run three hundred thousand miles—and if we run the car every day for one hundred miles, the service life of the chip will only be for three thousand days or eight years, two months, and twenty days. If the car only runs fifty miles every day, the service life of the chip will be sixteen years, five months, and ten days. The same is true with human sexuality. It is already known that a woman has thirty-six years of menstrual cycle. If she starts menstruating at age ten, she will have menopause at age forty-six; or if she starts at age sixteen, she will stop menstruating at age fifty-two. A woman is productive during the period from start to the end of her menstruation, but this does not mean she would lose her sexual desires because desires are regulated by the brain. She still responds to sexual stimuli until such time when her brain refused to do so. On the other hand, men's capacity to produce healthy seminal fluids that carry the sperms necessary for reproduction also has limitations. Theirs is rather different in the sense that youth and physical fitness determine the quantity and quality of the seminal fluids they ejaculate. The volume is more at younger age, gradually declining as they aged. The sperm also depends on the volume and temperature of the seminal fluids that protect them. There are men who could not produce healthy sperm because the volume and the temperature of the seminal fluids cannot hold the sperms up to the point of encounter with the female egg. Along the way, the sperm dies. Again sexual desires in men are also regulated by the brain until such time the brain refused to do so.

Applying the analogy of the electric bulb and the car chip, men who are promiscuous at an early age, having sex ten times a day, would surely have an early sexual retirement at age forty, not because of the brain refusing, but because the quality of the seminal fluids, the factors that control erection and ejaculation, diminishes as often as he discharged them. On the other hand, those men who are prudent and regulated in their sexual activities would probably still enjoy sex even at age eighty. This is also true with women who are promiscuous. They may have the desire to have sex but their body does not feel the pleasure anymore.

The human body being corruptible and subject to decay puts limitations to the desires of the flesh. Man will never have a lifetime enjoyment of sex. The reality of it could possibly be the reason why people want to enjoy it as much as possible and by any means. In view of this premise that humans are made out of matter and that matters are finite, the pleasure of sex is finite as well. Philosophers, theologians, and mystics told us that there is a sexual pleasure that is more than what we experience on the physical level. They call it spiritual orgasm, spiritual sex, or ultimate bliss. It is an experience that is heavenly and beyond sanity; this compelling desire to reach such experience made man restless. Saint Augustine of Hippo, who spent his younger days with lustful activities, said in his prayer to God, "You have made us for yourself, O Lord, and our hearts are restless until they rest in you" (Confessions of St. Augustine). He came to a realization that those who live according to the flesh are concerned with the things of the flesh, but those who live according to the spirit are concerned with the things of the spirit. The concern of the flesh is death, but the concern of the spirit is life and peace (Romans 8:5-6).

Part VI

Heaven: The Ultimate Answer

I am the way,

and the truth, and the life,

no one comes to the Father

but through me.

—John 14:6

The Invitation

*Come to me, all you who are weary and are burdened and I
will give you rest. Take my yoke upon you and learn from
me, for I am meek and humble of heart; and you will find rest
for your souls; for my yoke is easy and my burden is light.*

Mathew 11:28-30

In the conversation between Nicodemus, a Pharisee, a ruler
of the Jews, and Jesus Christ, Nicodemus wondered how Jesus
could perform acts that are of divine nature unless of course if
he is God sent or that God is with him (John 3:1-21). Jesus Christ
told him that no one can see the kingdom of God without being
born (from above) again. Nicodemus asked what does being born
again mean. Jesus presented his answer this way: "What is born
of flesh is flesh and what is born of spirit is spirit." He likened the
spirit with the wind that blows where it wills; the sound could be
heard, but no one would know where it comes from and where it
goes. If people find it hard to believe in earthly things; how much
more if they were told of heavenly things. He spoke of heavenly
things, such as God's love for mankind by sending his only son to
the world so that anyone who believes in him might not perish but
might have eternal life. God did not send his son into the world to
condemn the world, but that the world might be saved through
him. Those who do not believe have already been condemned
because they have not believed in the name of the only son of
God. Jesus Christ told Nicodemus what he sees in the world. He
is the light that came into the world, but the people preferred
darkness to light because their works were evil. Everyone who

does wicked things hates the light and does not come toward the light because his wicked works might be exposed. But whoever lives the truth comes to the light; he is not afraid to be exposed because his works may be seen as done in God.

To continue our journey to the afterlife, we are called to respond to the invitation of Jesus Christ to walk in the light of truth through our churches, congregations, and religious assemblies and to live our lives according to his teachings. The New Testament, which accounts for the ministry of Jesus Christ on earth, contained the Gospels, which means "the good news," telling the faithful that the kingdom of God is at hand and that Jesus Christ whom he sent will lead us the way. The Catholic faith, in her catechism, likened the relationship of Jesus Christ and the faithful as a marriage: Jesus Christ as the groom and the church his bride. In the miracle at the wedding at Cana (John 2:1-12), the identity of the bride and the groom was insignificant in the story. As told, Jesus Christ, together with his mother Mary, was invited. Three statements were emphasized in the story: Mary's concern that the wine is running short, Jesus' hour has not come yet, and the wine served in the wedding was kept good to the very end of the wedding celebration. Why should Mary and Jesus be concerned? They were only there as guests. What is the significance of their presence? Going back to the time of Adam and Eve, God said to the serpent after finding out Adam and Eve ate the forbidden fruit, "I will put enmity between you and the woman and between your offspring and her" (Gen. 3:15). God said this to the serpent because he knows that the weakness of the flesh is so compelling for a man and a woman to refuse or refrain, and that the devil would use this to manipulate them into committing sins; therefore, lose the inheritance of the kingdom that God originally had intended for them. Mary is the woman God promised and Jesus her offspring. For the family to be safe and protected from the snares of the devil, it is expedient that in marriage, a divine shield must be present in their union. The installation of the divine shield is expressed in the marital ceremony performed by a priest inside a church; in a civil marriage, the shield is not present. The first miracle happened before Jesus Christ could even begin his ministry. When Mary told Jesus that the wine ran short, Jesus replied that his hour has not come yet. How does Mary's concern affect him? Yet he did what Mary asked of him. The emphasis of this line in the story is that Jesus Christ will do what his mother would ask, even in emergency situation. Similar proof of his saving ministry was when he cured a sick man on a Sabbath (John 5:1-18). We can say that the wedding, a marriage ceremony, the binding of man and woman as husband and wife forming a family, is the foundation of a society and the wine that they shared together during the ceremony must be kept good throughout their marriage, but could only be kept good with the blessing of Jesus Christ and with the intercession of the Blessed Mother Mary. Why, of all things, it was the wine that ran out and not the bread or the fish. The wine, also called "spirit," symbolized happiness and merrymaking, and it also symbolizes the excitement in the sexual union. Wine also symbolizes the blood of Christ. In a marriage ceremony, the bride and the groom drink the wine in one cup. Jesus Christ is the living wine.

In the sacrifice of the Holy Eucharist, Jesus Christ invites all faithful: black, white, young, old, rich, poor, male, female, homosexuals, perverts, pornographers, pedophiles, prostitutes, sinners, and saints. The Eucharist calls us to justice. No more social distinction, everyone kneels and pray together. The Eucharist commemorates the death of Jesus Christ, offering his body together with the offering of the faithful, his bride, before God the Father, to bless the offering so that his body becomes the living bread and his blood the living wine for the faithful to have eternal life and be united with his Father in heaven. In the communion of the faithful, they share one bread and become one body with Christ; they drink one cup with Christ and become one in blood with Christ.

What kind of sacrifice must we offer in this gathering? The rich, to share his wealth to the poor; the pedophile, to give up his sexual liking for children; the homosexuals, to put an end to same-sex relationship; the prostitutes and pornographers, to give up their livelihood; the perverts, to make straight their manic behavior; and everyone who has issues on relationship with his family, neighbors, and friends. The word "sacrifice" in the dictionary means "a giving up of some cherished or desired object; to give up, yield, permit injury to, or relinquish (something valued) for the sake of something else, as a person, thing, or idea" (Funk and Wagnalls 1987).

A rich young man who claimed to have followed all the commandments of God, yet still felt wanting, asked Jesus what he must do to gain eternal life. Jesus told him to sell all that he had and give them to the poor. The young man went away sad because he had many possessions (Matt. 19:16-26; Mark 10:17-27; Luke 18:15). This is what Jesus Christ said to Nicodemus: that in order for us to enter the kingdom of heaven, we have to be born again in the spirit. Our journey to the kingdom of God requires us to be free from material attachment, including our misguided sexual desires. God does not condemn anyone who is weak in flesh. If the desire of the flesh corrupts the soul, then offer this in a sacrifice. The word here is "sacrifice," which means we give up something that we cherished, possessed, valued, enjoyed, and loved for the sake of something else. We cross oceans for sex; we climb mountains for sex; we kill others for sex; we debase ourselves or others for sex, and we even give up kingdoms for sex; it is ironic that we give up anything for sex, including our dignity, but not for the kingdom of God.

Jesus Christ came to this world to lead us the way to God's kingdom. He was telling us in his ministries to repent and make good our ways. He spoke in parables about what the kingdom of God is all about and how to get there. Through his Pascal sacrifice, he offers himself as the sacrificial lamb before God so that sins may be forgiven and many will be given the title to heaven or be heirs to the kingdom of God. Jesus Christ is offering us "eternal life" in the kingdom of God. Those who do not believe in him are already condemned and will have eternal damnation.

To believe in Jesus Christ and to live life in accordance to his teaching is a tall order for all of us. There are still people everywhere who stick to their own belief; they find flaws in Christian teaching, like they want it perfect in their eyes, or maybe they want Christianity tailored to their lifestyle. On the other hand, there are those who believe in Christianity but found it very difficult to follow that they just stay within the perimeters, enjoying life their way while waiting for judgment day, and then they will repent. For anyway, God is a forgiving God; he gives forgiveness to all those who ask for it, even at their deathbed.

The Ultimate Bliss

What has sex got to do with our final destiny, which is heaven? Why do we sometimes call a sexual experience "heavenly"? This concept had its beginning with the Greek in their mythology. The Greek gods made sexual contacts with the mortals. Zeus was said to have so many children with the mortals of his choice. This sexual encounter with Zeus was a "heavenly" experience to the mortals. Eros, the god of love known in other name as Cupid, was the son of Ares, the god of war, and Aphrodite, the goddess of love. Cupid's "DNA" revealed two contrasting emotions as we see in his parents: from his mother cupid got "love"; from his father, the god of war, cupid got "hate." This may explain why some relationships are described as having a "love-hate" nature. The love between man and woman was called *Eros* by the ancient Greeks. The Greeks considered *Eros* as a kind of intoxication, overpowering reason by a "divine madness," which tears man away from his finite existence and enables him to experience supreme happiness (Pope Benedict XVI, *Deus Caritas Est*). The Greek word "erotic" from Eros, the god of love, is used to describe a sensual feeling of tasting the "divine."

Long before Christianity, mystics from around the world came up with some form of enlightenment that served to answer their longing for perfect happiness or immortality. In China, great teachers such as Lao Tzu and Confucius influenced the Chinese people with their writings about their philosophy of life on how to attain frugality, joy of living, and simplicity. The common theme of Taoism and Confucianism was self-denial, self-knowing, and union with the ultimate. Practitioners of Taoism believed that by performing and following the discipline, one could stay in good health and eventually attain immortality. In India, Siddhartha Gautama, a prince who lived a life of comfort, luxury, and pleasure, saw the sufferings of the people outside his father's palace; he decided to renounce all of his material attachment and lived a life of austerity and discipline. He founded Buddhism as a way of life, practicing compassion for all living beings without discrimination and working for their good, happiness, and peace, to eventually develop wisdom, leading to the realization of the ultimate truth. Sexuality in Buddhism is just like any other behavior. If sexuality becomes a destructive behavior or the cause of one's problem in life, Buddhism teaches their followers to stop and correct the behavior. Sexuality in Buddhism can be moderated by awareness of its consequences and through meditation. Their teaching is more focus on self-discipline, wisdom, compassion, and enlightenment. It is in their belief that man would have to undergo reincarnation until he has attained the ultimate wisdom and compassion, which is termed "Nirvana" http://www.berzinarchives.com/web/en/archives/approaching_buddhism/world_today/intro, Introduction to Buddhist Sexual Ethics).

The Greek and Roman civilization also contributed their influence in man's endless quests for the ultimate. To the Greeks and the Romans, human sexuality plays a vital role in their daily activities and in their relationship with their gods. The Arabs, as well as the Persians, also made great contributions to man's search for eternal life here and beyond. Sexuality in Islam is second only to the service to Allah. Muslim men considered sex a privilege and women as a source of their pleasure. Once a woman becomes undesirable to a man, he can divorce her at will and take another wife. Man's search for spiritual awareness and immortality leads him to all form of beliefs, discipline, and rituals; sometimes his search leads him to the abyss of confusion, perversion, crime, and passion.

Some New Age groups practice a form of sexual discipline known as Tantra. Those who practice Tantrism reported to have experienced the so called spiritual sex. Although it aims to experience the union of the body and the spirit, the feeling stays on the personal level; it is only momentary. One criticism about Tantra is in its objective, which is a personal, self-help, with aggressive, non-loving sexual perversion. Tantra can be practiced as a group forming in circle, but the focus is on personal and spiritual discipline—to be in union with the divine or the "world soul" encapsulated in the image of the goddess Shakti. Another deity venerated is Shiva, a male-female god (http://www. newfrontier.com/nepal/tantra_enlightenment_through_sex. htm). The tantrikas believed that spiritual awareness can be achieved by controlling sensory experience. The Hindus in India also have their own version of Tantra, but most of them embraced the "Kama Sutra" expression of their sexual needs. Kama Sutra does not aim at achieving immortality. It is an artful expression of human sexuality aiming at achieving the highest excitement in the sexual act.

In Christian theology, man can find and reach his final destiny, which is heaven, by being born in spirit. In a conversation with Peter Seewald, Pope Benedict XVI was asked about why man is constantly searching for the meaning of his existence. He sums up his answer with one simple word, which is "love," that our life tends in the end to the discovery of love—that of giving and receiving love. Since God is himself love, it then is both a fundamental rule and the ultimate aim of life (God and the World, 185). God is the center of our sexuality, and relation of the sexes is the fiber of human existence (Pope John Paul II, Theology of the Body).

Mother Teresa responded to the invitation of Jesus Christ with all her heart in the service of the poorest among the poor in Calcutta, India. She saw the face of Jesus in the people that she served without condition, without complaining, without tiring. But no one knew until she died that there were moments in her life that she questioned God's existence and God's love. She called this her darkest moment because she saw nothing and felt nothing, like she just did not exist; but in the darkness, Mother Teresa found the answer to the longing of her soul. She saw her interior suffering, questioning God's love, as a "means of purification," and she surrendered to it. What Mother Teresa experienced could be explained in this way: If we stay in a dark room with our eyes closed, we see nothing; if we open our eyes, we see darkness around us. By opening our eyes, we become aware and conscious of our surroundings. The eyes is said to be the window of the soul; closing the window, the soul finds nothing; opening the window, the soul searches for something. It searches only the lights because the soul is part and parcel of that light it is searching. Once the soul finds the light, it experiences the ultimate bliss as it joins with the source of the light, which is God.

Mother Teresa of Calcutta wrote in her confession that there were times she believes God does not exist. She found herself walking in total darkness, not seeing a being at all. In her journey she thought there is nothing in this darkness. In this "darkness" moment of Mother Teresa, her material identity (physical body) was in the process of being born again and was undergoing a spiritual transformation. At the time of her death, she joined with "the Great Light" in perfect bliss.

There was no mention in Mother Teresa's book *Come be my Light*, how she dealt with her sexual needs. However, reading the book makes you understand that she considered Jesus Christ as her lover—a spiritual lover—always addressing him as "my love". Is this possible? Can a mortal express love to a spirit sexually? Some says that the intensity of such love could be expressed at its highest level of expression, just like having an orgasm, but the definition used in such experience is "like having rapture or in a trance". It has been observed that some mystics or saints "float" during the heights of their meditation—as in "levitation".

Beatific vision is a gift of actually seeing God face-to-face, and in this encounter we feel the ultimate bliss that we have been pursuing for all our life. The experience of actually seeing God face-to-face is likened as having an orgasm in a sexual intercourse. The physiological definition of the word "orgasm" is the swelling in an organ or part followed by subsidence. In common terminology, the word "orgasm" is a spasm of an organ. Actually, "orgasm" is the throbbing sensation felt as the swelling of the sex organs, caused by so much blood supply and excitement, begin subsiding. The keyword here is "throbbing," "pulsating rhythmically," or "palpitating." When a heart is overflowed with emotion or excitement, it throbs; the degree of excitement determines the pace of throbbing. In a sexual intercourse, the heart throbs faster than ordinary as the excitement heightens until the orgasm is reached, and then it subsides. Why do we compare the "ultimate bliss" with having an orgasm in a sexual intercourse?

Parables are short narratives, making a moral or religious point by comparison with natural or homely things (Funk and Wagnalls 1987). When Jesus Christ was proclaiming the "good news" called "the Gospels," he used parables to explain the kingdom of God. Most of the parables about God's kingdom and about relationship used stories about fishermen and workers in the vineyards. It was easier for the followers to understand the story if it is told using the casual day-to-day happenings of their lives. Most of the followers were either fishermen or workers in the vineyards. It is also in this line of reasoning that the writers of the sacred texts used sex and marriage as a comparison of how blissful God's love for mankind is. What other human activities could we think about to use in conveying to the people the ecstasy of seeing God face-to-face but the union of a man and a woman in marriage? Jesus Christ loves his church just like a husband loves his wife. In the "Song of Songs", Christians interpret this as the union between the groom representing Jesus Christ and the bride, his church. To the Jews, the groom is the representation of God; and the bride, Israel.

However, the use of the word "orgasm," as likened to the final encounter with god is not about the sensual aspect of the experience. It is the throbbing of the heart, the pounding of the heart as the passion heightens, the heart as the seat of human emotion, the heart as the center of love and compassion.

A sexual intercourse as an expression of love is the *dance of the soul*. While the physical bodies are connected passionately, the souls dance in unison as they become one. This dancing experience of the souls transcends human passion into blissful union, and having experience this together, their love becomes eternal and divine as the dance culminates into the bosom of their creator. The physical body is only an instrument used to express the feeling that resides in our hearts. The throbbing and pounding of the heart, as the souls dance into one, serve as the music that magnifies the intensity of love being shared together. In the miracle at the wedding at Cana, the wine at the wedding feast symbolized the intoxication of the bride and the groom as they savor and enjoy their sexual union. It was no ordinary wine; it was the wine blest by Jesus Christ.

We would be asking ourselves why sexual intercourse is the most exhilarating, most exciting, most amazing experience a man and woman crave so passionately. What do we get from this? Does the experience give man and woman the same level of excitement? We know the answer is no. Married couple, the unfaithful, the religious, the pedophile, the rapist, the serial sex criminals, the prostitutes, the pornographers, the perverts and addicts, the insane, the young, and the old experience different levels of sexual excitement; yet they all long for one thing more about sex. Some are happy to have it; some are deprived of it; some are unfortunate not to have it; some just could not find it. We all long for *love*: the feeling of loving someone and the feeling of being loved in return because we all know *love* connects us to the *divine*, the source of a love that is unconditional and outreaching.

Conclusion

The answers to the question does God really exist have been the topic of endless debates between believers and non-believers. Some great thinkers and Theologians argue that the creation of the universe which mankind could not claim authorship on its existence is a proof of God's existence. On the other hand, non-believers also point to the universe as the basis of their arguments that there is no such thing as a Supreme Being responsible for the existence of the universe; that its existence started with an explosion of its elements. Up to this time the arguments continue; each parties never conceding with each other's lines of thinking. One explanation why this kind of disagreements continues is the very fact that they believe they have the logic that can prove or disprove every line of arguments being presented.

Even before man discovered knowledge about the universe, the tribal days have given us the answers that there really is a God, a Supreme deity that mankind cannot live without. Their acceptance of the fact that they have no control of their own destiny and that only a supernatural being can perform or grant them their wishes led them to supplicate mercy, assistance, and guidance from this invisible being. Most of those tribal rituals and beliefs were sexual in nature. Perhaps this is so because their own sexuality had caused them so much confusion thus a great mystery to them. They would offer their prettiest virgin to appease this being; they would dance naked to ask for fertility; they would perform sexual offerings as a form of communication with this being—a crude belief that this being has the answers to the mysteries of sex.

We too have in our minds all sorts of questions regarding our sexuality. Why is it so compelling? Why even the old and the aged still crave for this? What has sex got to do with our final destiny which is heaven? Why even the religious people get in trouble with this? Why do we sometimes say our sexual experience is "heavenly"? These and all other questions need to have some answers or we would be subjecting ourselves to the desires and urges of our own physical body which sometimes go beyond our control.

God did not plan to banish mankind from his sight. He created them because of his desire to have company in his kingdom. When Adam and Eve disobeyed his commandment not to eat the fruit of the Tree of Knowledge of Good and Evil, he knew their future generations would experience the misconception about their own sexuality, even without the instigation and temptation of the devil, because the ground itself which man was made of follows the laws of nature. If this is so, what should mortals do with regard to his sexuality if it goes beyond normal needs and defies reason? In the Bible, God gave us the answers twice. When he made the covenant of circumcision with Abraham, he made mankind know that he is an essential persona in the reproductive activities of man, and again when Jesus Christ converted water into wine in a wedding at Cana, God through his son, Jesus, made mankind know that the best of wine—a symbolism of sexual excitement and marital bliss—served during a marriage is one that is blest by God. In the Bible we see how God played a vital role in the sexual lives of the people during those days.

When Jesus Christ was confronted by a mob chasing an adulterous woman, he was seen writing something on the ground with his finger. Theologians and many others have their own interpretations as to what Jesus Christ was writing about. In my point of view, he was not writing anything; he was pointing his finger to the ground to remind us that the ground holds the answer to our sexual desires and urges. In Genesis 3:17-19, God cursed the ground from which he made man because the ground by its very nature made man mutable—capable of multiplying, transforming, growing, evolving—or in other words "fertile". Man's body now becomes subject to decay, like all the others, and would experience death. Man becomes a finite being. But God breathe into man the soul of life, elevating him from among the other creatures, giving him the title to heaven and making him an heir to the kingdom of God. Man's destiny does not end in the graveyard; he has an afterlife—his final destiny.

Jesus Christ made it the center of his ministry while on earth the invitation to respond to his call for repentance to have an eternal life. When asked about fornication, marriage, divorce, and adultery, Jesus Christ said that these are the affairs of the flesh and the concern of the flesh is death. He made it clear in his conversation with Nicodemus that unless man is born again in spirit, man cannot enter heaven. He further said he was sent not to condemn the world but that the world would be saved through him.

Our sexuality led us to the abyss of confusion, addiction, perversion, insanity, crimes, and passion. Even if we have achieved the highest of sexual gratification, we still crave for more; we have that feeling of wanting to fill in a vacuum in our soul; a longing to connect and express our deepest desires—the desires of our heart which is to love and be loved in return. This is the mystery of our sexuality that can only be understood if we believe it is, according to the Greek, a "divine madness" that intoxicates human reasoning. Our earnest desire to experience supreme happiness or the ultimate bliss is the fulfillment of love in its truest and purest form as it connects to God—the source of an outreaching and unconditional love. This experience of supreme happiness is likened as having an "orgasm" in its indescribable heights; the endless pounding, throbbing, and palpitation of the heart as the soul unites eternally to its source—its creator.

Selected Bibliography and Related Readings

Augustine. 1469. *The Confessions of St. Augustine*. Translated with an introduction and notes by John K. Ryan, 1960

Bailey, Beth L.1989. *From Front Porch to Back Seat: Courtship in Twentieth Century America*. Maryland: Johns Hopkins University Press.

Cochini, Christian, SJ. 1990. *The Apostolic Origins of Priestly Celibacy*. San Francisco: Ignatius Press.

Crimes and Punishments: The Illustrated Crime Encyclopedia. 1994. 28 vols. Westport, Connecticut: H. S. Stuttman Inc.

Danielou, Alain, trans. *1994. The Complete Kama Sutra: The first Unabridged Modern Translation of the Classic Indian Text by Vatsyayana*. Vermont: Park Street Press.

Encyclical Letter: "Deus Caritas EST" of the Supreme Pontiff Benedict XVI.2005. Libreria Editrice Vaticana

John Paul II. 2003. *Reasons for Hope*. Ohio: St. Anthony Messenger Press.

Lewis, Dorothy Otnow, MD. 1998. *Guilty by Reason of Insanity*. Random House Publishing Group.

Lusterman, Don-David, PhD. 1998. *Infidelity: A Survival Guide.* CA. New Harbinger Publications, Inc.

Miles, Jack. 1996. *God: A Biography.* New York: Vintage Book.

Mother Teresa. 2007. *Come Be My Light: The Private Writings of the "Saint of Calcutta"* New York, Doubleday Publishing Group.

Ratzinger, Joseph Cardinal. 2002. *God and the World: A Conversation with Peter Seewald.* Translated by Henry Taylor. San Francisco: Ignatius Press.

Rawson, Hugh. 1997. *Unwritten Laws: The Unofficial Rules of Life as handed down by Murphy and other Sages.* New Jersey: Castle Books.

Rice, Charles.1999. *50 Questions on the Natural Law, What It Is and Why We Need It.* San Francisco: Ignatius Press.

Siegel, Daniel J. 1999. *The Developing Mind: How Relationship and the Brain Interact to Shape Who We Are.* New York: The Guilford Press.

Soble, Alan. 2006. *Sex from Plato to Paglia: A Philosophical Encyclopedia.* 2 vols. CA, Greenwood Press

Strange, Christopher M. 2008. *Brain in your Pocket.* New York: Metro Books.

Walsch, Neale Donald. 1996. *Conversation with God:An uncommon dialogue.* (audio book) CA. Audio Literature.

Walsch, Neale Donald. 2005. *What God Wants: A Compelling Answer to Humanity's Biggest Question.* New York: Atria Books.

West, Christopher.2005. *Created and Redeemed, the Universal Message of John Paul II's Theology of the Body.* A DVD presentation. Ascension Press.

West, Christopher. 2001. *John Paul II and Sacramental Sex: What Hollywood Doesn't Know and Your Parents Never Told You.* (audio book). CO: Our Father's Will Communications.

West, Christopher. 2003. *The Dignity of Man: An Introduction to the Anthropology of John Paul II.* (audio book) WY: Our Father's Will Communications.

Web sites visited:

Abiogenesis
http://en.wikipedia.org/wiki/Abiogenesis

Abrams, Rachel Carlton, MD. 2009.*Taoism and Sexuality*
http://womenshealth.about.com.od/sexualhealthissues/a/
taoismsexuality.htm

AbulKasem. 2009. *Sex and Sexuality in Islam*
http://www.sex-in-islam.com/abul.kasem/sex-sexuality-islam.htm

Anderson, Kerby J. 1992, *Pornography*
http://www.leaderu.com/orgs/probe/docs/porno.html

Australia
http://www2.hu-berlin.de/sexolgy/IES/australia.html

Family and Sexual Mores in Ancient Egypt
http://www.horemheb.com/sexuality.html

Ingram, R. Jackson Armstrong. *The Provisions for Sexuality in the*
Kitab-i-Aqdas
http://bahai-library.com/conferences/sex.aqdas.html

Introduction to Buddhist Sexual Ethics).
http://www.berzinarchives.com/web/en/archives/
approaching_buddhism/world_today/intro

Liberated Christians. 1997. *History of Sexuality in Cultures.*
http://www.libchrist.com/bible/history.html

Nimmons, David, *Sex and the* Brain. 1994
http://discovermagazine.com/1994/mar/sexandthebrain346

Now Public. *Ancient Pagan Sex Rites Practiced in Modern Times*
http://www.nowpublic.com/culture/ancient-pagan-sex-rites-
praticed-modern-times

Pederasty
http://en.wikipedia.org/wiki/Pederasty

Pornography
http://en.wikipedia.org/wiki/Pornography

Qazi, Shahid, Grisanti Carol, NBC News. March 24, 2009. *The*
'working girls of Quetta' — children
http//worldblog.msnbc.msn.com/archive/2009/03/24

Robinson, Marnia, and Wilson, Gary. 2005. *Your Brain and Sex*
http://www.reuniting.info/science/sex_in_the_brain

Sacred Prostitution.
http://en.wikipedia.org/wiki/Sacred_prostitution

Scientology and Sex
http://en.wikipedia.org/wiki/Scientology_and_sex

Scientology and Sex
http://www.scientology-lies.com/faq/teachings/sex.html

Scott, Shirley Lynn. 1999. *What Makes Serial Killers Tick?*
http://new.trutv.com/library/crime/serial_killers/notorious/tick/
victims_1.html

STD Statistics Worldwide. 2001. World Health Organization
http://www.avert.org/stdstatisticsworldwide.htm

Taoist Sexual Practices
http://en.wikipedia.org/wiki/Taoist_sexual_practice

Tribes
http://malkangiri.nic.in/Tribes.htm (The Bondas)

Virato, Swami Nostradamus, 1996. *Tantra: An Academic View*
http://www.newfrontier.com/nepal/tantra_enlightenment_through_sex.htm.

Walshe, M. O'C. *Buddhism and Sex.* 2006
http://www.accesstoinsight.org/lib/authors/walshe/wheel225.html

West Encyclopedia of American Law (Full article). *Pornography*
http://www.answers.com/topic/pornography

About the Author

Liberacion Tecson Paragoso is a certified public accountant and a retired accounting and auditing instructor for eighteen years. She lives in Houston, Texas. She is also a crafter, a fashion designer and seamstress, a food caterer, and an interior decorator. She has two children who are both accountants and who also live in Houston, Texas. She has written and published three books.

Other books by the author:

My Shoes and I
Funny and Sometimes Heartbreaking Experiences with my Shoes
(Xlibris, 2009)

The Origin and Semantics of Some Cebuano Words
(Xlibris, 2008)

Chosen: The Presidency of George Walker Bush,
The 43rd President of the United States of America
(Dorrance Publishing, 2005)